HEBREW
VERSUS
GREEK

HEBREW
VERSUS
GREEK

A DEVOTIONAL STUDY OF SCRIPTURE
THROUGH TWO LENSES

CHAIM BENTORAH
AND
CHRIS PALMER

WHITAKER
HOUSE

Boldface type in the Scripture quotations indicates the authors' emphasis.

Hebrew versus Greek
A Devotional Study of Scripture Through Two Lenses

www.chaimbentorah.com
www.chrispalmer.me
www.instagram.com/chrispalmer

ISBN: 979-8-88769-082-7
eBook ISBN: 979-8-88769-083-4
Printed in Colombia

Whitaker House
1030 Hunt Valley Circle
New Kensington, PA 15068
www.whitakerhouse.com

Library of Congress Cataloging-in-Publication Data (Pending)

1 2 3 4 5 6 7 8 9 10 11 WH 31 30 29 28 27 26 25 24

CONTENTS

INTRODUCTION ON HEBREW

Chaim Bentorah

For many years, I have been writing a blog in which I share a daily Hebrew word study in a devotional format. As with most blogs, there is a place where readers may comment. I often delight in these comments; some seek to share their personal insights or even attempt to correct an error I may have made. As a teacher, my goal is not to only impart information, but also make the reader think or even encourage them to do their own research on a matter. However, as a teacher, I do not encourage halfway thinking. As Alexander Pope once said: "A little learning is a dangerous thing." Every once in a while, someone will claim that they have *fact-checked* me and did not find any use of the English word that I used to apply to a certain Hebrew word. Hence, they conclude that I just made the whole thing up. People have also told me, "Oh, I have studied this word in the Hebrew, and it means..."

Normally, what these people mean when they say they fact-checked me or studied a word is that they just looked it up in a lexicon—and that's it. However, that is not all there is to a word study.

A rabbi once told me that there could be up to thirty-five possible English words for one Hebrew word. That does make sense when you consider that there are only approximately 8,500 known words in Classical Hebrew, approximately 7,500 words in Biblical Hebrew, and over a million words in English and an equal number in modern Hebrew. In addition, over five thousand new words are added to the English language every year while zero new words are added to Classical/Biblical Hebrew, a dead language. So we have a real challenge when deciding which English word to plug into a Bible verse, *especially* when we try to closely match that English word with the context of the Hebrew word and what was in the mind of the one speaking it. We also want to be sure we use a word that matches what God intended for our understanding in English.

This means that a translator must even consider the different nuances in English words, which are not the same for every individual. Hence a translator may translate a passage or word that fits his own world view and picture of God—one that gives someone else in some other part of the world an entirely different picture than the one the translator had in mine.

How is a translator supposed to choose from all these various possible English renderings and still convey the same idea that he has to someone who may have a greater or lesser depth of understanding for an English word? To be sure, the Holy Spirit plays a prominent role in this decision, but the translator will also use other tools to bring it about. This is why a translation must be a team effort. No one should attempt to create a Bible translation alone other than for personal use. A Bible translation must involve a team of consultants with knowledge of the culture and the period that the passage was written. They must have a background in archeology, anthropology, and linguistics and be well versed in the language from many different sources.

Thus, I have partnered with another student of God's Word and biblical languages who has expertise in examining not a major translation of the Bible but just a few key words.

There is something that is commonly overlooked by many attempting to translate the Bible from the original Hebrew, and that is examining the four thousand years of wisdom and knowledge of the people of the Bible. The Jewish people are the masters and guardians of the Hebrew language. Their libraries are filled with insights into its development. This is something that many Christians, including pastors and Bible teachers, have not even begun to consider.

If one seeks to fact-check this dusty old professor, they will need to do more than look up a word in a lexicon, for my sources include archeological discoveries of ancient cultures as well as the teachings of Jewish sages and rabbis in the Midrash, the Talmud, and the Targum, along with Jewish commentators such as Rashi.

We use another highly valuable source in this book to give a deeper understanding of a word in Hebrew: the Septuagint or LXX, a translation of the Hebrew Bible into the Koine Greek. The value here is that the translation of the Septuagint predates the birth of Christ. It was the work of Jewish scholars within a couple hundred years after Classical/Biblical Hebrew became a dead language.

Classical Hebrew became a dead language during the captivity period around six hundred years before the birth of Christ. During this time of exile, the Jews adopted Aramaic, the language of their captors and a close cousin of Hebrew. During the postexilic period, many Hellenistic Jews adopted the Koine Greek language, and Hebrew simply became ceremonial language, much like Latin is in the Catholic church. Many Jews were unable to read, write, or even speak the Hebrew language. Thus, an attempt was made to put the Hebrew Bible into the language of the people. The result was the Targum, an Aramaic version of the Old Testament. This was really more of a paraphrase than an actual translation but it still reflects the thoughts and idioms of that period.

During this time, the Greek pharaoh of Egypt, Ptolemy II Philadelphus, sent seventy-two Jewish translators—six from each of the twelve tribes of Israel—to Alexandra to translate the Old Testament from the Hebrew to the Greek because he wanted a Greek version of the Jewish Tanakh for his library.

Traditionally, Christian scholars have used the Masoretic text that was copied, edited, and distributed between the seventh and tenth centuries AD as their primary source for our modern translations. However, recent discoveries from the Dead Seas Scrolls have suggested that the Septuagint, translated hundreds of years earlier, carries a higher degree of accuracy than the Masoretic text.

Our knowledge of the Classical Hebrew and Koine Greek is increasing thanks to discoveries in modern archeology. It is felt by the authors of this book and their publisher that the time has come for a collaboration on a book incorporating all of these disciplines.

INTRODUCTION ON GREEK

Chris Palmer

The idea of working on a Hebrew/Greek word study devotional was as much exciting as it was daunting.

Exciting because few such books, if any, exist.

Daunting because few such books, if any, exist.

The initial conversations between me, Chaim, and the publisher centered around the idea of how we might pull this off…or at least try.

The challenge was twofold:

- First, the obvious challenge: The Old Testament is written in Hebrew, and the New Testament is written in Greek. How does one do a word study from both? Normally, you pick a word from either testament, discuss it from the original language, and draw an application. Not so with a Hebrew/Greek word study. That's a bit more complex.
- Second, the not-so-obvious challenge: While Chaim and I have both written word studies, we differ in our methodologies.

Chaim has elaborated somewhat on his method already so I will touch on mine. My hermeneutical and exegetical training consist of critical methods. In my work thus far, I have used both the historical/grammatical method (*Letters from Jesus, Greek Word Study,* and *Strange Scriptures*) and the narrative method (*Winks from Scripture*). The historical/grammatical method examines the syntax of the language as well as the historical context in order to determine what the original author was saying and how the original hearers would have heard it. The narrative method looks at stories in the text by examining various elements such as plot, characters, conflict, and point of view in order to determine how the original audience would hear these stories and what effect this storied theology would have on the listeners.

How would we work together with such different methods?

The first thing we determined was that we would respect each other's methods. He could use his, and I could use mine.

The second thing we realized was that in order for a Hebrew/Greek word study to be possible, we would have to start with a passage from the Old Testament and see if that passage had any connection to the New Testament through a word or phrase, relying on the Septuagint or the LXX, so named for the seventy Jewish scholars who translated it.

Chaim would begin the study from the Hebrew Bible, using his method to discuss what the Hebrew word meant. Then I would examine that particular word or phrase in the LXX. If the word or phrase the LXX used to translate the Hebrew word was in the Greek New Testament, I'd look to see if there were any peculiar connections. Perhaps a New Testament passage is echoing the Old Testament by choosing the same Greek word that the LXX has used. (This happens quite often.) Or perhaps the New Testament author's use of a particular word has been informed by the various nuances of that word established in the LXX. (That happens pretty regularly too). Finally, we also decided to pay attention to what is called *intertextuality*—the way in which one text informs another.

Let me give you an example. Say I am writing a story about a husband and wife, and they're talking on the phone. The wife is a heart surgeon, and she tells her husband she has to go because she has to do an operation in an hour. The husband ends the call by saying, "Well, I hope the force is upon you." If you grew up in the 1970s and '80s, you'd get this because you would know that he is alluding to *Star Wars*. Although it's not a direct quote from *Star Wars*, it's certainly informed by those movies. What gives us suspicion is the word *force* and how the husband is using it. This is intertextuality. and it is one of the things we used to bring passages and words in the Old Testament together with passages and words in the New Testament through the LXX.

So what you will find in the following studies is Chaim starting with a Hebrew word from the Old Testament and me using the LXX as a bridge to how that word is used in the New Testament. Throughout this book, we both add illustrations and applications to make our research practical.

I realize that this might not be on par with the critical methods that you have used in the past to study the Bible. Or maybe there's *too much* thought given to critical analysis of the text, or at least more than what you're used to.

However, I do feel that a book such as this, which attempts to examine the text through the use of various methods, is a good step in the right direction to discover what the Holy Spirit is saying to us. By respecting each other's methods and allowing one another to use the text in the ways that we've learned, I think Chaim and I have written something here that brings together academic scholarship, the human soul, and the heart of God—a good balance of a great combination.

Finally, a bit of a nerdy confession here. In 2021, I attended a Koine Greek conference at the Southern Baptist Theological Seminary. One of the keynote lectures was on the importance of incorporating the use of the LXX into Old and New Testament studies. In my own handling of the LXX in both my master's and doctoral work, I had felt this to be true. This lecture convinced me that the LXX is, without a doubt, underappreciated and underused in our theological pursuits, especially in working with the biblical languages. At a minimum, this book you are holding breaks ground by making use of it as an important tool for something as simple as a devotional Bible study. It is our hope that more biblical resources will utilize the LXX.

Last but not least, we sought to keep the applications in this simple and aimed toward themes related to knowing the Lord and walking with Him.

What you hold in your hands might not look much different from other devotionals, but different it is. It is a unique hybrid, a Hebrew/Greek word study forged with various methods by a Hebrew scholar and a Greek scholar using the Old Testament, the New Testament, and the Septuagint.

Daunting as it was, it was well worth the labor.

We hope you enjoy it.

1

GOD REPENTED?

*And it **repented** the Lord that he had made man on the earth, and it grieved him at his heart.*
—Genesis 6:6 (KJV)

Genesis 6:6 is one of those verses that gives us reason to pause. God … repented? This comes as a surprise. Why does a perfect God need to repent? What did He do wrong? Doesn't that go against what we know about the perfect nature of God?

We can get at the conundrum this verse presents by examining the word *repent*.

The Hebrew word *nachach* has its origins in the process of making pottery. Have you ever watched a potter at work, a truly artistic potter who never accepts his first product? He puts the clay on the wheel and fashions his vessel while the wheel spins. You may think that what the potter fashions is beautiful and adequate, but if it is not quite the way the potter wants it, he will smash it down and start over. He may fashion a number of vessels and smash them down before he has one that is exactly what he wants.

The word *repent*, as it's used in Genesis 6:6, becomes more interesting when it's examined in the LXX. Typically in the LXX, *nachach* is translated into Koine Greek as *metanoeo*, a word that usually defines our understanding of *repent*—"to change one's mind," often because one has been convicted of sin or wrongdoing. This is how the New Testament uses the word *metaneo* most often as well. (See Luke 15:10; Romans 2:4; 2 Corinthians 7:10.) Yet in Genesis 6:6, a different Greek word is used: *enthymeomai*. This word means "to consider" and "to ponder." In Matthew 1:20, *enthymeomai* is used to describe Joseph's reaction when he discovered Mary was pregnant: *"But as he **considered** these things, behold, an angel of the Lord appeared to him in a dream."*

The pondering this word describes is never without emotion, oftentimes sorrow. And that's precisely what is going on in Genesis 6:6. With sadness, God pondered what His creation had become. The potter noticed his creation had some pretty hefty flaws in it. He was brokenhearted, perhaps the way we might imagine Joseph's heart was broken when he initially discovered that his betrothed was pregnant with a child that wasn't his.

What adds to our understanding of Genesis 6:6 is its placement in the story. You may recall that in Genesis 1, God first created humankind. Seven times, God looked at His creation and called it good. (See verses 4, 10, 12, 18, 21, 25, 31.) The joy, elation, and splendor of such a picture is emphasized by the seven uses of the word *good*. It was completely good! But by Genesis 6, God's creation has become sinful, broken, and lost. And God pondered what had taken place with a broken heart.

So God, as a creator and potter, didn't regret that He fashioned or created humankind. He acknowledged, with heaviness, that some impurity had entered. Sadly, to remove it, he would have to start over.

However, the last phrase in Genesis 6:6—*"it grieved him at his heart"*—moves the illustration to a higher level than just a potter forming a vessel. It shows the potter having a relationship with that vessel and doing all he can to perfect it before smashing it down and starting over. Dennis Prager, an orthodox Jewish talk show host, gets this right when he renders this phrase as "and God was sad." God was sad that the corruption of sin had brought pain and suffering to the innocent.

The *Mona Lisa* was Leonardo da Vinci's masterpiece. He spent a lifetime painting it. He was constantly reworking bits and pieces of it. He would sometimes stare at it for hours and then make a slight alteration to a certain brush stroke. He cherished the portrait, nurtured it into existence, and spent a lifetime perfecting it, making it look just the way he wanted. Can you imagine what da Vinci would have felt if he returned to his studio one day and found some vandal had entered and splashed paint over his *Mona Lisa*? That would surely have "grieved his heart" and made him sad. The word *grieve* from Genesis 6:6 in Hebrew is *atsab,* which means "to be sad" or "to travail." When God saw the failure of His people to be what He created them to be, when He saw an enemy come in and vandalize His masterpiece that He labored to perfect, His heart was sad and began to travail.

Interestingly enough, the word *grieve* is in a Hithpael form in Hebrew. This form indicates to us that God allows or causes Himself to grieve or travail over humankind. He doesn't *have* to have a broken heart, but He loves us so much that He will allow Himself to suffer the pain of a broken heart over our failure. This is evident throughout the entire story of the Bible. Yet no other place in Scripture compares to the suffering we see demonstrated in Christ as He hung on the cross as a sacrifice for humankind to become a new, holy creation.

God does not meet His creation's rebellion with a cold detachment. He allows His heart to break. He puts us back on the potter's wheel. He works us toward perfection by eliminating that which grieves Him.

Have you recently done something that grieves the Lord? The bad news is it has grieved Him. The good news is He pondered over it with care and affection. And now you are on the potter's wheel. The stab you feel might simply be the working out process that every masterpiece must undergo.

Pray this from your heart:

Lord, You grieve over my sin. Place me on Your potter's wheel until I am pleasing to You, my Creator.

2

GOD'S UNIQUE LOVE

To the Chief Musician. A Psalm of David the servant of the Lord, who spoke to the Lord the words of this song on the day that the Lord delivered him from the hand of all his enemies and from the hand of Saul. And he said: I will love You, O Lord, my strength.

—Psalm 18:1 (NKJV)

Our English word for *love* has become a matter of perception. In our Western culture, we have used the word so carelessly it has lost its real significance. We love our parents, our friends, our pets, our cars, our burgers, and our Spotify playlists. Advertisers love us, politicians love us (especially in November), and we don't have to go far to if we need someone to tell us that they love us—just drop a dollar bill in that guitar case, and the busker on Las Vegas Boulevard will tell you that he loves you. You might go into a Starbucks and hear the manager tell the customers, "We *love* you!"

Hmm.

No wonder when you approach someone and say, "God loves you," you get a, "Yeah, that's nice, sure thing, okay, glad to hear it, big deal, so does that guy who's always singing 'Sweet Caroline' next to the Bellagio hotel."

But if someone were to say, "God cherishes you," or "God honors you," you might respond, "Wow, really?"

In truth, our English word *love* was originally meant to express something like *cherish* or *honor.* Yet love is so overused that sometimes we need to substitute those words in order to get our point across.

Some years ago, Chaim was working in a halfway house and found it more effective to say to one of the residents, "Hey, I really respect you" rather than, "Hey, I love you." To those troubled individuals, the word *love* had lost all its meaning. They heard the word used in so many different contexts that they had no idea what anyone was talking about when they said, "I love you."

Because of this, we must be specific about what we mean when we say *love*. For instance, we can watch a romantic movie in which the handsome young hero takes the young woman in his arms. Tenderly he looks into her eyes. Just before touching her lips with his, he whispers, "I love you." There's a big difference between that and that same old boy biting into a Big Mac, smacking his lips, and telling the sandwich, "I love you."

As Christians mature and grow closer to the heart of God, they begin to realize how cheap and insignificant the English word *love* is compared to the emotion they began to feel and receive from God. On its own, *love* is simply not enough. People who grew up in a loving home may speak of parents who loved each other and got along in beautiful harmony. They speak of a father who never looked at another woman and could never imagine their mother even thinking of another man. They often do not say that their parents loved each other but instead say they *cherished* each other. Why not use the word *love* to describe the feelings this couple had for each other? Because it's not good enough. Therein lies the problem in expressing the emotion that we experience with God as we draw closer to His heart.

We need an English word to describe this love, but it seems that no one can come up with something that is greater than love. So most of the time, people usually add an adjective to the word love, like "abiding love," "parental love," "childlike love," or "unconditional love."

Biblical languages can help us out here.

Let's examine Psalm 18:1 (NKJV) where David says, *"I will* **love** *You, O Lord, my strength."*

Ahav, the usual Hebrew word for love, and *chav,* the usual Aramaic word, are quite adequately rendered as *love*. However, Psalm 18:1 does not use the Hebrew word *ahav* but another word for love, *racham*.

Now it is easy to say, "Well that is just a synonym like we have in English." Both *ahav* and *racham* seem to be used interchangeably. The problem is that when you have only about 7,500 words in the Biblical Hebrew and 8,500 in the Classical Hebrew, it seems unlikely that two entirely different words would have *identical* meanings.

The word *racham* is found forty-seven times in the Hebrew Old Testament. It can be defined as "to love" and "to have compassion." It is found once in a Qal (simple verbal form) in Psalm 18:1 used by David to say, "I love You, Lord." The remaining forty-six times it is found in the Hebrew Bible, it is in a Piel (intensive) form used by God to express His love for us.

This would suggest that our love for God is on a human level and could not match the love God has for us. Think of the greatest love of your life—be it a spouse, a child, a parent, or even a friend—meditate on that love, and then try to image a passion greater than that. Still, you cannot imagine the depth of God's love for us, for if you could find it somewhere in the Bible, it would have a human expressing *racham* to God in a Piel form.

The *Brown–Driver–Briggs Lexicon* shows the word *racham* is used for softness and gentleness.

The *Davidson Analytical Lexicon* tells us that *racham* is used to express the idea of loving tenderly.

Rabbi Samson Raphael Hirsch, a nineteenth-century linguist and Hebrew master, indicates that *racham* is protection from harm.

In the Aramaic of the Targum and Talmud, the word is identical in spelling as *racham* and is used to express the idea of befriending someone, becoming a friend. It is also used to convey the idea of stimulating maternal instincts and nursing a child who is not one's own. It is also an extreme love and expressed in English as, "I love you with all my heart" or "with all I possess."

In the Akkadian language used by the Assyrian Empire in the cuneiform, *racham* is found to be used for a mother's womb, which denotes a mother's care.

So, how does the Greek treat *racham*? In the Greek Septuagint, the word *racham* in Psalm 18:1 is translated as *agape*.

In pre-biblical Greek, there are a number of words to describe the word *love*, including *phileo, eros,* and *agape*. *Eros* describes sensual intoxication. It is a tyrannical desire that overtakes an individual and forces them against their will. It was to be conquered lest one be seized by it and act against one's better judgment. Interestingly enough, this word is never used in relation to God's love toward man or man's love for God. The biblical texts completely disassociates from this idea for its presentation of God's love.

Instead the biblical texts look to two other words to describe God's love: *phileo* and *agape*. *Phileo* is an earnest, loyal love—noble, faithful, and steadfast. Imagine the disposition you have toward a dear friend you've been in battle with, one with whom you've shared warm, salty tears. The other word, *agape,* is often used in association with honor and esteeming someone over yourself. These words are often used as synonyms in the Greek, as is the case in John 21:15–19, where Jesus and Peter have an exchange about Peter's love toward his Lord. Peter affirms his loyalty, honor, and preference for the Lord after having denied the Lord during His passion.

Together, *agape* and *phileo* both lend to us the idea behind the Hebrew *racham*. They describe a loyal, steadfast love that prefers others first. Peter, who had previously failed Christ, was renewing his love toward his master. It's not too much of a stretch to hear the restored Peter echoing David here: "I will love Thee (*racham/agape/phileo*), O Lord, my Strength."

While we can *love* our Big Macs, trips to Whole Foods, favorite athletes, and L'Oréal cosmetics, let's make sure we know that the *love* we have for God is something special, deeper, and far from casual. It's *racham, agape/phileo*. No human disposition runs deeper than that.

Pray this from your heart:

I will love You (cherish You, remain loyal to You, and prefer You above all else, with all I possess, O Lord), my strength.

3

WELDED TO GOD

I will say of the Lord, He is my refuge and my fortress: my God; in him will I ***trust.***

—Psalm 91:2 (KJV)

The psalmist is giving us the simple secret to finding a refuge in God and making Him our fortress. It is found in that word *trust*. Now how much simpler can you get? We throw this word around all the time as Christians. *Trust* is one of those Christian audibles that we use when we are desperately trying to comfort a loved one who is going through a trial. Suggesting that we need to place our trust in God is excellent, biblical advice, but somehow, when we share it, we feel that we have failed to adequately offer comfort. Why do we feel that way, and why is the person we seek to comfort not always encouraged by this advice? Perhaps it's because these words have become a cliché to us—and we never stop to think of what it means to *trust*.

Let's consider some American history for a moment. On July 30, 1956, the 84th Congress passed a Joint Resolution, approved by President Dwight Eisenhower, that the United States adopt the words *In God We Trust* as the official motto of our country, replacing *E pluribus unum*—Latin for "out of many, one"—which had been adopted in 1782. "In God we trust" was the battle cry of the 125th Pennsylvania Infantry on September 17, 1862, during the Battle of Antietam, one of the bloodiest battles of the Civil War. *In God We Trust* first appeared on U.S. coins in 1864 and on paper currency in 1957.

In 1956, despite efforts by atheist groups, the House of Representatives passed an additional resolution reaffirming the motto by 396–9. A 2003 Gallup poll showed that 90 percent of Americans support the inscription of *In God We Trust* on coins.

So here we have trust in God as the foundation of American society. It's so familiar and it's everywhere. Yet when things become too familiar, they become unfamiliar, and things that appear everywhere often seem to be nowhere. How many U.S. citizens know what it means to *trust in God?*

The Hebrew word for *trust* used in Psalm 91:2 and elsewhere in the Bible is *batach,* which means to "adhere to." It is the word for *glue* in Modern Hebrew, but it originally came from the ancient art of welding. In fact, *batach* is the ancient word for welding. Welding has been traced back to the Bronze Age beginning around 2,300 BC and evidence of welding has been discovered in the Mesopotamian area as early as 1,500 BC and 1,000 BC.

When you weld two pieces of metal together, the point where the weld is formed is said to be stronger than any other point in the entire piece of metal. You can break that piece of metal anywhere else before you ever break it at the weld. This process is what the ancients used to describe the idea of *trust*. When we *trust* in God, we blend and melt ourselves into Him and He into us with the heat intensity of God's *racham* love and our love for Him. When we trust in God, we will never break in any area of our lives that is welded to Him. The only way to guarantee that an area of your life does not break is to weld it, blend it, into God or *trust/batach* it to God.

In the LXX, the Hebrew word *batach* gets translated into the Koine Greek word *elpizō*. The proper meaning of this word conveys the idea of confidence. In fact, it is such confidence that it produces the expectation that we will not be let down. In the New Testament, *elpizō* is mostly translated as *hope*. Perhaps the best example of this is found in 1 Timothy 5:5. Here, Paul is writing to Timothy about taking care of the widows among the community. He qualifies widowhood by saying that a widow is one who has been *"left all alone"* and *"has set her hope on God and continues in supplications and prayers night and day."* In other words, she is helpless and has no one to take care of her. In this stranded state, she must *"set her hope"* (*elpizō*) on God. Given what we have learned, a picture starts to form of a widow who begins to weld herself to God through confident trust, in total hope that God will take care of her and not let her down. As she regularly prays and supplicates, the weld gets stronger.

Welding is often used in the construction of modern skyscrapers, bridges, and other metal structures rather than riveting, which was common in the past. Welding makes the buildings sturdier and more able to withstand any storms or earthquakes. A weld is the strongest of attachments—two pieces of metal, fused into one.

Perhaps the lonely widow who welds herself to God can teach *us* a lesson or two. In our helplessness, we need to fuse ourselves to the Lord with confidence and trust. In these uncertain times, having *In God We Trust* as our motto and our mindset is beneficial for our country, the church, and individuals. The next time there is civil distress, disorder in your church, or personal crisis, remember to treat your helplessness by creating a brand-new weld. We can join those stranded widows in heartfelt prayer until our confidence fuses us to God, who won't let us down.

Pray this from your heart:

Helpless as I am, I turn to You, Lord, with my prayer. May it weld me to Your divine power so that in You I might trust.

4

COMMANDED NOT TO FEAR

Have I not commanded you? Be strong and courageous. Do not be frightened, and do not be dismayed, for the Lord *your God is with you wherever you go.*
—Joshua 1:9

Fyodor Dostoevsky (1821–1881) was a Russian writer who suffered from epilepsy and had a very hard life. He became a civil engineer and secretly wrote novels. His first novel, *Poor Folk*, was published in 1846 and was a commercial success. However, three years later, in 1849 at the age of twenty-eight, he found himself before a Russian firing squad. Dostoevsky received a last-minute reprieve and was sent to a Siberian labor camp, where he worked until he was released in 1854. He was then conscripted into the Russian army, where he fought on the Mongolian frontier. He returned to Russia in 1859 and started a magazine at age thirty-eight. In 1864, his wife of seven years and his brother both died, the magazine folded, and Dostoevsky found himself deeply in debt. In 1866, he published one of his most popular novels, *Crime and Punishment*. Although a classic today, it did not bring in enough income to pull him out of debt. His novel *The Brothers Karamazov*, published in

1880, finally brought him financial success, but Dostoevsky died a year later, before he could enjoy it.

Dostoevsky was a man whose life was filled with fear and dismay. He coped with his fear by analyzing it as a writer and philosopher. Writing of his travels in Western Europe, he said, "Try to pose for yourself this task: not to think of a polar bear, and you will see that the cursed thing will come to mind every minute." This is the very thing we all attempt to do when we face a difficult or trying situation.

Say you are facing a medical test to determine if you have cancer. The moment the doctor mentions the test, you begin to worry and fret; you are fearful. You cannot concentrate on anything but that upcoming test and the results. You manage to put it out of your mind for a moment by some distraction, but the moment the word *cancer* pops in your mind, you can't help but think about it and worry anew.

Joshua 1:9 is a strange verse when you think about it. Can someone literally be commanded to be strong and of good courage, to not be afraid or dismayed? When one thinks of the word *command*, they think of receiving an order. Yet the moment someone tells you not to be afraid, the word itself becomes Dostoevsky's polar bear, and you become afraid again.

Joshua and the people of Israel were going to face war and all the terrors of war. There would be casualties; it would be bloody, horrifying, and terrifying. How can one not fear in the face of war? It is a natural emotion. Nelson Mandela once said, "Courage is not the absence of fear but the triumph over it." In other words, true courage is not being unafraid, but moving forward despite fear.

The people of Israel were commanded not to be afraid, to be of good courage. But if courage is moving forward despite fear, how can one be courageous and not fearful at the same time? In Hebrew, the word *courage* is *'amatz*, which means "to be obstinate, firm and steadfast." Despite our fears, we are to stand firm and steadfast. But then we are commanded to be not afraid. The word Hebrew word for *afraid* is *'aratz,* which is so closely related to *'amatz* that it suggests a play on words. It can mean to "be terrified" but it has a causative nature to it. Don't cause yourself to be terrified by being *'amatz,* standing firm in your *'aratz,* which also means to be focused and decisive.

Again, can one command another to be focused? We can encourage someone to be focused but we cannot command it. However, this word *command* in Hebrew is *tzavah,* which really means "to give a charge or give authority." In other words, God is not commanding us to be of good courage or not be afraid; He is giving us the authority to be courageous and not fearful. Authority is the power or right to give orders. We are given the power to order our minds to focus on God and the mission He has given us.

As many people grow older, they find themselves fretting over their declining health. They become fearful of losing their ability to function normally. They live in fear of losing cognitive ability or the ability to perform essential tasks such as taking a shower or walking up stairs. Every time they bend over and feel arthritic pain, they become fearful because that pain is just like Dostoevsky's polar bear, a reminder that disability and even one's ultimate demise may be just around the corner. They become fearful and in dismay over what the next weeks, months, or remaining years will bring.

But if you are a believer in God, you are reminded that your sojourn on this planet is in His hands. Joshua 1:9 tells us that God has given you authority over this negative, fearful mindset, that He is your Creator and that every day He gives you to live on this planet only brings you into a closer relationship with Him. He gives you the authority to overcome these fears when you focus on His Word. Then when you bend over and feel that pain in your back, you are no longer in despair of your life coming to an end but you rejoice over the years He has given you. The future only promises a closer walk with Him until you enter into His arms, and He ushers you into your eternal home with Him forever.

Coming over to the New Testament, we see this play out in the familiar story of Jesus walking on water in John 6:16–21. When New

Testament writers wrote the accounts of Jesus, they almost always had Old Testament Scripture in mind. This is especially true of John. He always tells his stories of Jesus in parallel with something from the Old Testament, echoing those Scriptures and alluding to those stories. If you aren't seeing the accounts of Jesus paired with the Old Testament, your readings could use more dimension and scope. In John's account, Jesus's disciples see Him walking on the water, and they are "*frightened*" (verse 19).

The Greek word for *frightened* is *phobeō*. This is the same word that the LXX uses in Joshua 1:9 when God commands Israel not to be dismayed. The word means "to be shattered with terror." Today we might say "to become unglued." Something is so frightening that it smashes our resolve into little bits and plucks our courage. Imagine having a nightmare. You hear yourself screaming in your sleep. You wake up in a cold sweat and grapple to find the light so you can turn it on and make it all stop. This is the sort of fear we find in Joshua 1:9 and John 6:16–21. It's likely that Jesus is alluding to Joshua 1:9 when He commands His disciples *not* to be afraid. When John tells this story, he wants the reader to think of the two events together. And then Jesus tells them why: *"It is I."* The God of creation has drawn near. Doesn't this sound like the encouragement God gives the Israelites in Joshua 1:9, "*for the Lord your God is with you wherever you go*"?

The power and authority that God has given us to command and order our minds so that we are not afraid is possible because *"It is I"* is with us. He has drawn Himself near to us in moments of fear so that we don't have to come unglued.

This reminds Chris of a conversation he had with his friend Rachel, who lost her father suddenly when he had an unexpected heart attack. Rachel's father was her best friend; before his death, her Instagram was filled with pictures that showed daddy/daughter dates, tributes on Father's Day, and her dad giving her away at her wedding. Not long after he passed, Chris asked Rachel how she dealt with the tragedy. She replied, "From the time I got the call that my father had left us until now, I have had an unexplainable peace. I know it sounds cliché. But it hasn't left me from that time until now." God's presence had given Rachel the authority she needed to remain pieced together for one of the worst, imaginable tragedies of life.

We have ample opportunity to catastrophize, to allow worst-case scenarios to roar at us and make our knees feel rubbery. When Dostoevsky's polar bear shows up, remind it that you are not afraid. *"It is I"* has drawn up next to your boat. You can be strong and courageous for the Lord God is with you wherever you go…even into that polar bear's den to face it square on.

Pray this from your heart:

Courage is found in You, Lord, my God, who commands me to order my mind so that it remains fixed on Your goodness and power.

5

HAVE WE HEARD IT SAID THAT WE CAN HATE?

*Do not I **hate** them, O Lord, that **hate** thee? and am not I grieved with those that rise up against thee?*
—Psalm 139:21 (KJV)

Reading this verse in English can give us a very unsettling feeling. Every translation uses the word *hate*. We have heard sermons in which we are told to hate those who hate God, and Psalm 139:21 is our proof that we are given the right to do so.

On various news media, we hear and see protesters shouting in the streets and even in the chambers of Congress against certain laws or individuals. We may not understand a word they are saying but we can feel the hatred. You listen to reporters interviewing someone with an opinion different than theirs and despite their attempts to appear to be impartial, you can still feel the hatred. Chaim recalls hearing a reporter defend himself after one hateful exchange; he said he was just trying to get a question answered. It was obvious this was not the case because there was literal hatred being expressed. The media kept playing this exchange over and over. One could get physically sick listening to this hatred.

Hate is such a horrible, negative emotion. People who are filled with hate suffer many physical and mental disorders. Hate only creates more hate and division. What did that hateful exchange between the reporter and the person being interviewed really accomplish? Afterward, those who sided with the reporter were gleeful, thinking the person who was interviewed got his comeuppance, while those who sided with the interviewee only expressed more hateful rhetoric.

Psalm 139:21 seems to give us a green light to hate those who hate God. Religious zealots and cults take this verse to the bank. They stand outside of churches, funerals, and just about any event you can think of, telling everyone that God hates them. And that *they* hate them too! Obviously this is wrong; just look at 1 Peter 3:9. But what do we do with Psalm 139:21?

Should we just ignore it as something that we are unable to understand? Declare, as many do, that the Old Testament has no relevance to us today as those books are filled with anger and wrath whereas the New Testament is filled with love and forgiveness? God forbid we become a Marcionite and infer that Jesus is different than the God of the Old Testament! Are we to say we live in a new dispensation today and the teachings of the Old Testament are no longer applicable to us? Or might we just conclude that God is a moral monster?

Many of us believe the whole Bible is relevant to us today, that every word is meant for us. We devote our lives to studying both the Old Testament and the New Testament.

To further this dilemma, there are some would who say that the Quran teaches hatred toward those who do not follow its teachings—and yet does not Psalm 139:21 teach the same thing? Muslims worship the God of Abraham, Isaac, and Jacob, but they view Him in a much different light than Christians do. Thus, they hate the view of God that we worship. Does Psalm 139:21 instruct us to hate them in return?

Perhaps the problem is wrapped up in the English word *hate,* which means "to dislike intensely or passionately." We have no problem intensely disliking the exchange between a reporter and someone with an opposite viewpoint during an interview. We have no problem intensely disliking the political demonstrations that accomplish nothing but create division. That fits our English definition of *hatred*. We use the word *hate* in many different contexts. We hate eating liver. We hate rainy days when we are on vacation at the beach. We hate Facebook. In other words, we have an extreme dislike for these things. We say that, and others sort of smile. Yet if we were to say we hate an individual, that creates a negative emotion. If we say we hate the way that individual behaves, the negativity is not so strong. Hence, the word *hate* is a very rudimentary and confusing word.

The Hebrew word used in Psalm 139:21 is *sana'*, which is the Hebrew word for *hate*. However, as our English word for *hate* is inchoate, we really need to consider the emotional context that this word is used in and maybe consider an English word that expresses that context. In some cases, the English word *hate* expresses a very negative emotion and reaction from others; in others, such as "I hate liver," there is no outrage.

The nineteenth-century Hebrew master and linguist Rabbi Samson Hirsch applies the English word *rejection* to *sana'*. He does not even apply the English word *hate* to *sana'*, being very mindful of the emotion behind words. As our English word *hate* creates a negative emotion in most cases, he steers away from the emotion when using the word in the context of God.

Rabbi Hirsch's discretion is merited when considering Matthew 5:43. Here, Jesus is giving the Sermon on the Mount, and He gets to that famous part where He tells His audience to love their enemies. His lead into this is, *"You have heard that it was said, 'You shall love your neighbor and hate your enemy.'"* Hmm. The Greek word for *hate* is *miseo*. It has a range of meanings but here, based on the context, it means "to hate" or "to detest." So just *when* did they hear it said that they should love their neighbors and hate their enemies? Nowhere in the Old Testament, that's for sure. Scholars are quick to point this out. Since we find this instruction nowhere in Scripture, what Jesus is likely referring to is the inference that people get from Scriptures like Psalm 139:21. Like many of us, they were misunderstanding it too! Perhaps their vitriol toward their enemies was boiling over so much that they were looking for anything in Scripture to justify their hatred. Jesus puts an end to that. As the God who wrote the Scriptures, He interprets and states quite clearly that humanity is not allowed to hate in the evil sense of the word.

Now, consider a real clue to the emotion behind *sana'* in Psalm 139:21 (KJV). This is found in the fact that this verse is a couplet. The psalmist, King David, repeats the same thought in a different way. In the first part, he says, *"Do not I hate them, O LORD, that hate thee?"* In the second part of the couplet, he clarifies what he means by hate: *"And am not I grieved with those that rise up against thee?"* Now he is saying he is grieved by those who rise up against, or, rather, *reject* God. Another feature of this verse that adds to the meaning behind it is the word *grieve*. In Hebrew, it is the word *qot,* which is used here in a Hithpael form. Thus it would mean that the psalmist has a deep disquieting or loathing within himself that accompanies this act of rejection.

So it is technically accurate to render this passage as, "I hate them, O Lord, who hate You." But is better understood emotionally if it is rendered, "I feel a deep unsettling, sick feeling for them who hate You." That way, the next time you hear a reporter with whom you disagree, you can simply reject them with a sense of loathing by turning the TV off instead of conniving evil thoughts in your heart toward them.

Pray this from your heart:

I will turn away from those who do evil; I will loathe those who have turned away from You. And, yet Lord, I won't forget those for whom You died; I will show them the love You've shown me.

6

OLD, DIRTY RAGS

But we are all as an unclean thing, and all our righteousnesses are ***as filthy rags;*** *and we all do fade as a leaf; and our iniquities, like the wind, have taken us away.*
—Isaiah 64:6 (KJV)

We often hear an evangelist preach on Isaiah 64:6 and listen to him dramatically describe filthy rags, even showing us examples, holding up filthy, oily, greasy, muddy, shoe-wiped rags straight from a mechanic's shop. He waves them around and declares that all our good works, our church attendance, and our tithing are nothing more than filthy rags. We might as well hold these up to God as our ticket to heaven. We most certainly cannot deny that it's true; indeed Ephesians 2:8–9 clearly tells us that it is by grace we are *"saved through faith"* and *"not a result of works, so that no one may boast."*

Still, it is a little problematic to consider that all our good works are filthy rags. Is that to say it does not matter whether we are good or bad? That going to church, teaching Sunday school, or paying tithes are all meaningless filthy rags?

Well, let's examine just what is really being said here. This word for "filthy rags" in the Hebrew is *yebeged ʻidim. Yebeged* comes from the root word *beged,* the word for a *garment,* not a rag. To us, a rag is just an old piece of cloth used for dusting and cleaning. A *beged* is sometimes rendered as a *robe* but most often it means an inner garment—more specifically a lap garment or a garment that covers your lap or genitals. The next word is the one where we get the idea of *filthy*. *Idim* comes from a Semitic root word found in an ancient Persian word *'ed*, which means a period in the sense of "a reoccurring incident." By the time it reached the Hebrew, it meant menstruation. This filthy garment is really a garment worn by women during menstruation.

So, the garment itself is really not filthy in its original state but is in fact clean. Yet it is a garment that has been made unclean. Menstruation, according to Jewish law, causes a woman to enter into a state of uncleanliness. So the picture the prophet is drawing here is that our good works, our acts of righteousness, are not filthy; they are clean, they are worthwhile, and do bring pleasure to God's heart. In the context of this passage, it is referring to the Jews who followed a righteous path, followed all the laws of God, performed all the ceremonies, kept and honored the feasts but they did it just for ceremonial purposes, to win God's favor, to bribe God. In other words, with the wrong heart and with poor motives. This attitude caused these righteous acts to become unclean.

All our good works—going to church every Sunday, teaching a Sunday school class, paying our tithe—can really be abominations to God if they are used for selfish purposes, to try to win favor with God, perhaps persuade Him to grant some prayer request, or done in the hopes that God will say, "Well, how about that?! Now I will reward you greatly."

To look at this another way: You can learn a lot by sitting outside and tossing peanuts to squirrels.

You take a seat by a tree and suddenly, you are aware that you are being watched. It is a little gray squirrel on his hind legs, twitching his nose at you. Eastern gray squirrels do not hibernate but rarely come out of their den during winter to forage. They usually stay huddled together in their den, but on occasion, it is not unusual to see a gray squirrel in the dead of winter sneak out of his den in search of some food. You hold up a peanut. He scurries up a tree, but you can tell he is looking down at you. So you grab a handful of nuts and toss them on the sidewalk…only to have them land on a grassy area covered by new fallen snow. They are buried, and you figure your furry tailed friend will not see them.

However, the little beggar is undaunted. He runs down the tree and with his two little paws, he scrapes back the snow and then picks up one of the peanuts. He holds it in his paws and chews on it in stop-and-go fashion, all the while looking up at you. After he polishes off that peanut, you toss him another. This time, the little guy moves a bit closer to you. He digs past the snow, nibbles on the peanut, and looks up at you as if to say, "Thank you, got any more?" Each time you toss him another nut, you aim just a little bit closer to you. Then he begins to talk to you.

What, you don't talk to squirrels? Admit it, we all talk to squirrels; we just don't expect them to answer. Yet when you listen with your heart, you might begin to hear what they are saying, which is something like this: "I didn't want to get closer to you but if I am to get my peanut, I must get closer."

Our Creator is pretty much telling us that we are treating Him like that little squirrel treats us. If we don't need any peanuts, we are satisfied to keep our distance, but in the dead of winter, we may need all the nuts we can get, so we suddenly start to draw closer to Him.

Like our furry friend, we tend to only get close to God when we need Him to feed us. How nice it would be if that cute little rodent would just come up to us to say, "Hi." We would not have to coax him with a peanut because he needs a handout. If he wasn't hungry, he would not even give us the time of day. We can talk plenty about miracles, prosperity, healings, inner joy, and peace. Perhaps we are like squirrels who gather around God in the wintertime only because He has peanuts, and our supply is getting low. Without those nuts, we would not even delight Him with a twitch of our nose. He must pay out a peanut just to get a cute little gesture from us. Yet, He desires that simple contact with us a million times more than we long for a simple contact with that cute little bit of God's creation.

To close, let's have a look at the LXX. Here we will discover that the Koine Greek term for "filthy rags" *is rhakos apokathemenes.* While this phrase isn't used in the New Testament, Mark 1:9–11 certainly makes use of Isaiah 64, which is thought of as a post-exilic lament that mourns Israel's sinful state. Isaiah recalls the exodus and asks God to "*rend the heavens and come down*" to the people of God to heal their sinful state (Isaiah 64:1; see also Exodus 19:18–20). This motif is at the foreground of Mark 1:10, where the heavens rip open and the Spirit descends on Jesus like a dove. This indicates that the prophet's prayer has been answered. God was contacting His creation; He was coming to heal their sinful state and make them righteous.

Isaiah 64 and Mark 1 teach a few important lessons that speak to our relationship with God. First, we are deeply sinful and broken when left to ourselves. Second, our motives for doing good works can be quite sketchy. Our good works are filthy if we do them for the wrong reasons. But third, Scripture tells us that God has acknowledged our sinfulness and has come to reconcile us to Him in order to give us a new heart so that the motives behind our works can be pure.

Pray this from your heart:

I acknowledge my brokenness, Lord, and that the motives of my heart are not always true. Craft my intentions so that I approach You without guile.

7

THE LAUGH OF WONDER

Therefore Sarah ***laughed*** *within herself, saying,*
After I am waxed old shall I have pleasure, my lord being old also?…Is any thing too hard for the Lord*?*
—Genesis 18:12, 14 (KJV)

When Sarah overheard God telling Abraham that she was going to have a child at the age of ninety, she laughed. The Hebrew word used here for *laugh* is *tsachak*. Lexicographers have debated the nature of this word to determine what type of laughter Sarah had. Was it mockery? Was it just the idea of a ninety-year-old woman having a child? Was it the laughter of unbelief? Joy? Only the context will tell and even that is cloudy. So we are stuck with man's best guess as to what type of *tsachak* Sarah had. What are some of these *best guesses?*

Here is one for your consideration. God's response in saying that nothing is too hard for Him suggests that it was a laughter of unbelief and possibly mockery. Ah, but mockery at what? That is the rub. The Hebrew word translated as *hard* is *pala'*, which is in a Niphal form. It may be more correctly rendered as "a wonderfully hard thing from the Lord." It may also not even be in an interrogative (question) form at all. We will explain that later. The Hebrew word translated as *thing* is *devar,* which is usually rendered as "a word spoken from the heart." So here, it refers to a word spoken from God's heart.

What makes the syntax so difficult here is the fact that there is no verb in this sentence. You can do that in Hebrew but you can't do it in English. So we rely on the context to determine what verb to apply to make the sentence grammatically correct in the English language. Translators do this by making this an interrogative phrase and using the verb *is*. Chaim is not certain that the sentence needs to be in an interrogative form, but like most people, he likes the rhetorical question and is inclined to just keep it that way. What he does find disturbing is that the preposition *from* in front of God's name is not in the English translation.

A more appropriate rendering would be, "Is anything more marvelous or wonderful than a Word from God's heart?" As the interrogative is uncertain, we could also render this as, "There is nothing more wonderful than a Word from God's heart." This implies that any expression from God's heart is not *too hard* to perform. There is an old Scottish saying about a little girl carrying her disabled brother. When asked if he was too heavy to carry, she replied, "He na heavy, he's mi brother." When you perform a difficult task from your heart, it is not difficult at all.

Now let's look at that word *laughter*. It is the word *tsachak* spelled with three Hebrew letters: Sade, Cheth, Qop. The Sade shows humility and submission to God. The Cheth speaks of a joining with God, while the Qop whispers to us that we are going to have a new beginning with God. The Sade and Cheth would suggest that Sarah was laughing with God not at God. God had just let her in on His private joke that would confound the world. The word here would suggest that this laughter springs from the "joy of the Lord, the joy of a new beginning." Perhaps her fear at admitting that she was laughing was the fear that her laughter was out of context. When Sarah overheard God tell Abraham she would have a child, she submitted herself to this "Word from God's heart" and in doing so was so filled with the joy of the Lord that she broke out laughing, but then stopped herself because she felt her laughter was not appropriate. Keep in mind that Sarah was not a part of the conversation, she was eavesdropping, and in Oriental culture, she should not have been listening to the conversation of the two men. When God pointed out her laughter, she denied it. Not to deny it would be admitting to breaking protocol.

Have you ever found yourself suddenly filled with the joy of the Lord while praying? You begin to laugh, just laughing out of pure joy from the assurance that the Lord has everything under control. Then, maybe you stop yourself because you feel that you are not being reverent before God. Perhaps like Sarah, you just had a moment of faith and hope that God would take care of everything, and then you get hit with reality and the wisdom of man. Suddenly you are overcome by that wave of doubt that comes as reality sets in like it did for Sarah when she realized she was too old to have a child. God then reminded her that He had given her a Word from His heart, a promise that comes with an ironclad guarantee. Maybe we can read this as God not rebuking Sarah, but encouraging her to laugh, to continue to laugh with the joy of His wonderful promise. "Is anything more wonderful than a promise or Word from God?" God's response, *"No, but you did laugh"* (Genesis 18:15) is more appropriately rendered as, "No, just keep laughing."

Maybe that is why God said to name the child Isaac. *Isaac* is the same word as *tsachak (laughter)* only it has a Yod in front of it. The Yod puts this into an imperfect or incomplete action. Isaac was just the beginning of laughter that would continue for these two parents.

The word *laughter* in Genesis 18:12–14 in the LXX is from the Koine Greek word *gelaō*. Chris used a pretty effective pneumonic device to remember this vocabulary word in his first Greek class: "I laugh when I get gelato." He pictured himself in his favorite gelataria, tucked right next to the Trevi Fountain in the heart of Rome, getting handed a gigantic double-scoop of amarena gelato. His eyes grew as big as a pizza pie, full of wonder that within seconds, that soft creamy wonderfulness would send him into another orbit somewhere far from Rome. That's *amore*! But this pneumatic device was especially effective because the picture it painted was on par with the definition of *gelaō*: "be merry," "rejoice," and "make glad." Not only did *gelaō* sound like gelato but gelato brings *gelaō*! There was no way he'd forget this word. We bet you won't either.

In Luke 6:21, Jesus tells His disciples, *"Blessed are you who weep now, for you shall laugh"* (*gelaō*). The idea of *gelaō* here means to leap for joy. Perhaps it recalls how John the Baptist leaped for joy in Elizabeth's womb in Luke 1:41 when Mary, who was pregnant with Jesus, came to visit her aunt. If that's the case, then it's not going too far to suggest the motif of laughing for joy in both cases recalls how Sarah became alive with joy upon hearing that she would have a child.

Chris recalls a time in his own life when he experienced the laugh of wonder. He had read a book about praying specific prayers. It was quite adamant about searching one's heart in order to discover what is there and then offering those desires to God in supplication with precise, detailed prayers. Chris went on a walk and discovered there was a tremendous desire in his heart to preach in Italy. He wanted to go and minister in his ancestral homeland. He prayed, "Lord, I have this desire to preach in Italy, specifically Sicily. My ancestors are from there, and there is nothing more that I'd like to do than bring them the Word of God." Chris never really thought this prayer would get answered anytime soon. He didn't even know anyone in Italy—nor did he know anybody who knew anybody.

About two months later, Chris got a random email from a woman in Sicily who was the secretary of a pastor who presided over a number of churches. This pastor wanted Chris to speak at a church camp in Palermo, Sicily, for an entire week. Chris laughed with wonder and joy! Then he discovered that the camp was twenty miles from his great-grandparents' hometown, and he laughed even more. A few months later, he was on a beach in Sicily, looking at Isola delle Femmine and laughing because God had answered his prayer and answered it so quickly. He handed Chris a scoop of glistening amarena gelato. And Chris leapt with joy.

The laugh of wonder. Who knows the next time God will perform something so wonderfully hard that it will make you laugh with Him because He's let you in on His private little joke?

Pray this from your heart:

Let me in in Your secrets, Lord, that I might laugh in wonder at the wonderfully hard things You do.

8

VIOLENCE FILLED THE EARTH

O Lord, how long shall I cry for help, and you will not hear?
*Or cry to you "**Violence!**" and you will not save?*
—Habakkuk 1:2

Now the earth was corrupt in God's sight,
*and the earth was filled with **violence**.*
—Genesis 6:11

The word for *violence* in Hebrew is *chamas,* which has extremely broad usages. You may find some sources that spell this word *hamas,* which sounds an awful lot like the terrorist group in the Middle East. Oddly enough, in Hebrew, it means "violence," but the name Hamas is not a Hebrew word. It is an Arabic acronym for Islamic Resistance Movement. There is no evidence that the original organizers of the Hamas movement intended to make a word play off the Hebrew word *chamas.*

The Hebrew word *chamas* does speak volumes without its coincidental resemblance to the terrorist organization. In fact, *violence* might not be the best word for us to use here. This would be particularly true with its use in Habakkuk 1:2 and Genesis 6:11. *Chamas* expresses the idea of wealth or pleasure that is obtained through not only violence but also oppression, theft, intimidation, threats, lies, fraud, and other means to rob people of their personal possessions and wealth. This includes predatory lending, Ponzi schemes, and corrupt businessmen who put others out of business to enhance their own. It includes any corrupt means of government to obtain funds, like allowing a lottery to move beyond a game to become an act of desperation for people. It even includes those who obtain abortions so they can pursue their own selfish lifestyles. Ultimately, it carries out the idea of enhancing one's own power, wealth, or pleasure at the expense of another person. *Chamas* involves little things such as overcharging for your services or even using your social media platform to assassinate someone's character and reputation.

Chamas would also apply to using a promise of God's blessing as a tool to enhance your own power or wealth base, by encouraging someone to *chamas* by giving an offering to literally bribe God into giving you more in return rather than encouraging one to give from a sacrificial heart of love.

Today, the average person would not think any of these were violent acts. A common definition of *violence* is behavior involving physical force with the intent to hurt, damage, or kill someone or something. Yet, the aforementioned *chamas* acts are unjust and unreasonable.

The Greek word for *chamas* in the LXX is *adikia*. This word begins with what is called an "alpha privative." This is the letter alpha, our English "a," in front of a word for the purpose of negating what comes after it. And what comes after it is the word *dikē* or "justice." So *adikia* means "injustice" or "no justice whatsoever." Think flat-out twistedness, or a lack of respect for the dignity of another that enables the wrongdoer to take all that they can get without consequence. It's manipulation and guile.

Adikia is most commonly translated as "unrighteousness" in the New Testament. In Romans 1, the apostle Paul is describing the human condition and is diagnosing the world's problem as sin. Paul does something he is famous for—he gives a list. Pauline lists contain some of the most robust theological takeaways in all the epistles. There are little gems in every Pauline list!

> *They were filled with all manner of unrighteousness, evil, covetousness, malice. They are full of envy, murder, strife, deceit, maliciousness. They are gossips, slanderers, haters of God, insolent, haughty, boastful, inventors of evil, disobedient to parents, foolish, faithless, heartless, ruthless.* (Romans 1:29–31)

Whew! That's a lot of sin right there, isn't it? In looking at these verses, you are staring face to face with the disease that lives in mankind. It is like looking at the cancer on the X-ray. Notice what is at the forefront of that list—unrighteousness (*adikia*). In Pauline lists, the first item is usually one of importance because it introduces the list. It is sort of the beginning point. You could even make a case that the other items derive from the first one. Or you could make the case that the other items further describe the first item. Be that as it may, this list is distinguishing *unrighteousness* as the source of the cancerous actions. Paul could have even had in mind the state of the world in Genesis 6, when it was filled with *violence*.

Again, it's not that everyone was running around with a AR-15 rifle and shooting each other. This wasn't *The Purge*.[1] Rather, everyone was treating one another without dignity. They failed to see the image of God in one another. In doing so, they treated each other like things and possessions, having no fear or respect for the divine image in all of us. So it was more than unsafe streets and home invasions. It was people, often rich or powerful, taking advantage of other people, usually the weaker ones—the elderly and the poor.

---

1. *The Purge*, directed by James DeMonaco (2013; Universal Pictures).

In Habakkuk 1:2, the prophet cries to God, asking Him why He allows all this *chamas* or *adikia* to continue. Habakkuk was prophesying to Judah during the time of Jeremiah, which was just before the Babylonian conquest of that nation. The governmental, business, and religious leaders of Judah probably inflicted bodily harm on the people. But the real problem was taking advantage of the poor and unfortunate. People were starving, dying for want and neglect due to the selfish desires of the rich and powerful. Habakkuk calls out to God, asking how long people must endure this terrible treatment at the hands of the godless.

God says He has prepared an answer to Habakkuk's prayer. He was preparing a coming judgment to fall on the nation. There is an old saying that we may get tired of hearing but have to admit is true: "Be careful what you pray for." God tells Habakkuk that not only has He answered the prayer, but just how He was going to deal with this *chaman* or *adikia*. He was preparing the Babylonians to overpower Judah; they would kill, rape, steal, plunder, and destroy the nation. Many would die, all would be destitute, they would starve and be homeless. Most have been under oppression already, so this would be business as usual. But the leaders who enjoyed prosperity by exploiting the weaker ones faced the brunt of God's judgment. Their nation, one of the most powerful and wealthy in the world, would be reduced overnight into a Third World country.

Revival would come, although not quite the way Habakkuk wanted. Why should the just and righteous have to suffer along with the *chaman* (*adikia*) makers? God explains in Habakkuk 2:4: *"But the righteous shall live by his faith."* Well, that is not much of an answer until God brings Habakkuk to this realization:

> *Though the fig tree should not blossom, nor fruit be on the vines, the produce of the olive fail and the fields yield no food, the flock be cut off from the fold and there be no herd in the stalls, yet I will rejoice in the Lord; I will take joy in the God of my salvation.*
>
> (Habakkuk 3:17–18)

Even if tragedy or destruction falls on a nation, a church, or a family, God will bring joy to the faithful. And really, isn't joy in the midst of trials better than sorrow, pain, and depression in the midst of plenty?

One of the joys of Chris's ministry has been having good friendships in the Turks and Caicos Islands ninety miles north of Haiti. He's been teaching in the churches there for over a decade. Haitians outnumber the indigenous people of Turks and Caicos by three to one, according to Chris's pastor friend. They go there to escape the living conditions in Haiti. Chris's friend talked about the history of Haiti and gave his take on why it is so corrupt. This friend is deeply spiritual and a charismatic. He believes in demons and the reality of witchcraft, as do the authors of this book. But he feels that it is incorrect to say, as many Western charismatic Christians do, that Haiti is corrupt solely because it is given to witchcraft. Its corruption, according to him, has to do with its sad history. In 1804, Haitian slaves overthrew their French slave masters and declared their independence. Yet two decades later, the French returned and demanded payment and repatriations from the people it enslaved. They had to pay 150 million francs, a debt that could have been used to build infrastructure, schools, and hospitals. It was either pay this debt or go to war. Experts have calculated the cost of this debt and suggest it would equal up to as much as $115 billon over time. This has been a major contributor to the poverty in Haiti. The French government tapped Haiti for all it had. And this is only *one* of its economic dilemmas.

Our purpose in mentioning this is not to get into politics, but to use a modern example of what the violence of Genesis 6:11, Habakkuk 1:2, and Romans 1:29–31 looks like. It is people doing other people wrong—most often, the strong subjecting the weak to horrible conditions.

While you may not be in a position of government to change policy and we cannot go back and change history or even make up for all the injustices that have been done, we *can* treat humans with dignity, remembering that all of us are created in the divine image of God. *This* is righteousness. And it's the antithesis of violence.

Pray this from your heart:

I desire righteousness, Lord, my Maker and Creator. May I flee from the violent, those who pervert Your ways.

9

WONDERS ON BOTH SIDES

And the Lord *said to Moses, "Behold, I am coming to you in a thick cloud, that the people may hear when I speak with you, and may also believe you forever."*
—Exodus 19:9

If a prophet or a dreamer of dreams arises among you and gives you a **sign** *or a* **wonder***, and the* **sign** *or* **wonder** *that he tells you comes to pass, and if he says, "Let us go after other gods," which you have not known, "and let us serve them," you shall not listen to the words of that prophet or that dreamer of dreams.*
—Deuteronomy 13:1–3

Moses was one of the most important prophets in Judaism. Like most prophets, Moses performed signs and wonders. There is a big difference between a sign and a wonder. In Hebrew, a "sign" is the word *oth* from the root word *'avah*. It means a communication in expressing or communicating a desire. A road sign communicates a direction or a certain destination. If it's something you desire, you pay attention. If you saw a road sign advertising a certain tavern or bar down the road, you would ignore that *oth* or sign unless you were interested in stopping for a beer. If you saw a sign advertising burgers and fries, you might pay attention if you are hungry. So too, if a prophet comes along and offers a *sign* of something that you desire, you start to pay attention. The prophet may be expressing a healing, a glimpse into the future, or a possible word from the Lord that you may feel you need. This would be an *oth*, a sign, if it is directing you to what you desire. The prophet's words are a sign from God that He may be giving you your heart's desire.

Then we have a *wonder*. That is the Hebrew word *mopheth* from the root word *yapah*, which is also the same word for *beauty*. It may also be a miracle, but the Hebrew word for *miracle* is *nas*. *Yapah* is something that excites your senses and causes you to be in awe of someone or something.

To be sure, Moses performed many signs—that is, he directed and led people to what they and God desired. Many of these signs were spoken signs, words from the prophet, who said, "*Thus says the* L*ORD*" (Exodus 9:13). Moses also performed many wonders, bringing water from a rock, bringing plagues upon Egypt, and the granddaddy of all wonders, parting the Red Sea.

Who would not listen to a man like Moses when he spoke with such authority and performed such wonders? Yet the Mishnah, the Oral Torah, tells us that the people did not believe in Moses because of the signs and wonders. They thought someone could say anything that they wanted to hear, and those wonders could be trickery or sorcery. Besides, all the miracles Moses performed were of necessity. The splitting of the Red Sea was necessary to help Israel escape from the Egyptians and destroy the Egyptian army. (See Exodus 14:26–29.) The splitting of the earth to swallow up Korah and his crew was necessary to establish Moses's authority. (See Numbers 16:31–32.) But that was not the reason people listened to Moses.

Many Christians who have attended some conference or listened to a guest speaker in their church claim they witnessed what they felt were outright miracles, or the speaker told of miracles that occurred in his ministry. People automatically accepted whatever this speaker said because, after all, only a true man of God can perform miracles and surely no preacher who stands on a pulpit would lie or exaggerate miraculous claims. Yet, history is littered with stories of miracles from people who laid no claim to God Jehovah. How can we be sure the enemy, who is a master illusionist, is not performing some form of trickery, as Moses faced with the Egyptian magicians? A miracle is not a confirmation that someone is a true prophet or man of God. In fact, Jesus warns us that in the last days, many people will be deceived by wonders performed by false messiahs:

> *For false christs and false prophets will arise and perform great* ***signs*** *and* ***wonders****, so as to lead astray, if possible, even the elect.*
>
> (Matthew 24:24)

The Greek word for *wonders* here comes from *teras*. This means something unusual that produces excitement. This is the word that the LXX uses to translate the word *mopheth*, which means *wonder* or *portent*, like in Deuteronomy 13:1. Jesus was explaining that deceitful leaders would be listened to all the more if they could offer unusual happenings that excited their audience into action.

Yet this was nothing new. Kings in ancient times often had to create the illusion of being a god or endowed with power from the gods. They had to create a *yapah* or *wonder* about themselves. The pharaohs actually declared themselves to be gods and led people to believe they caused the Nile River to overflow to irrigate their crops. They proved it by predicting the exact time the Nile River would overflow every year.

In *The Wizard of Oz*,[2] the wizard had to create the illusion that he was great and powerful. However, when Toto pulled that curtain aside, Dorothy and her friends found just a friendly old con man who held his kingdom together with a lot of bluff and bluster. So too with the great pharaohs, who had a staff working behind the scenes, studying the

2. *The Wizard of Oz*, directed by Victor Fleming (Metro-Goldwyn-Mayer, 1939).

movement of the stars and doing mathematical calculations to predict the seasons.

A *wonder* or *yapath* or *teras* is simply an event, a statement, an act, or anything that would create a sense of awe in others. While Jesus warns us that they will be performed by wicked leaders, Moses's life also confirms to us that godly leaders perform them also. It takes discernment to know the difference, and it takes maturity not to throw the proverbial baby out with the bathwater. In other words, just because false messiahs have performed wonders doesn't mean we should discard anyone else who performs them.

God forbid we become like the skeptics who have challenged God's genuine servants who have performed wonders in His name. For instance, some thought George Müller had a couple pegs missing when he said he would start an orphanage without asking for any money and just trust God for the finances. Over a lifetime of ministry, Müller launched multiple orphanages that cared for more than 10,000 children. Madame Guyon was called a mystic and imprisoned in the Bastille for no other reason than the fact that she declared she loved Jesus and spoke with Him, and that God spoke with her. George Whitefield was barred from being a pastor because he dared to say that you can have a personal relationship with God, and that the poor and destitute should be allowed to worship God in a church. Really, isn't it obvious that these people were crazy? (We hope you can tell that we are being sarcastic.)

As twenty-first century Christians, we face a road with ditches on both sides. The first ditch is the temptation to go blindly after anyone performing, or claiming to perform, a wonder without realizing what wonders equate to one being sent from God. On the other side is the ditch of skepticism that makes us think that anyone performing a wonder is not from God simply because some who perform wonders are malevolent and deceptive. We need discernment and maturity to walk in a straight line and not get caught in either ditch.

Pray this from your heart:

Lord of wonders, give me discernment and maturity so I can recognize the wonders You perform through Your servants. May the wonders You perform captivate me and may I see through those wonders that are not from You.

10

CAUSE YOURSELF TO MOURN

It is actually reported that there is sexual immorality among you, and of a kind that is not tolerated even among pagans, for a man has his father's wife. And you are arrogant! Ought you not rather to ***mourn****? Let him who has done this be removed from among you.*

—1 Corinthians 5:1–2

Then Ezra withdrew from before the house of God and went to the chamber of Jehohanan the son of Eliashib, where he spent the night, neither eating bread nor drinking water, for he was ***mourning*** *over the faithlessness of the exiles.*

—Ezra 10:6

There appears to be a strong relationship between the passage in 1 Corinthians and Ezra in the sense that mourning over the transgressions of others will remove these transgressions from your midst or presence.

Chaim recalls a time when he worked as a counselor in a Christian halfway house. One young man was just released to the house after serving time in prison on a drug charge. He told Chaim that he had now been off drugs for over two years. Asked about his motivation, he said his wife was a Christian who prayed daily for him, crying out to God for his soul's salvation, weeping and mourning over his wasted life. One evening, he returned home and found his wife again on her knees by their bed, pleading with God over his soul. He said he was so high, he was literally out of his mind. Seeing her crying and mourning over him made him so angry that he grabbed her and punched her in the stomach as hard as he could. She fell to the floor crying out in pain, yet still pleading with God to forgive him. He then said from that point forward, he could never even touch any illegal drugs. He planned to spend the rest of his life doing whatever he could to make it up to his wife and God for the way he broke their hearts. He not only recognized that he broke the heart of a woman who dearly loved him but also the heart of God, who loved him even more.

To become aware that your actions are breaking the hearts of the ones you love is probably the greatest motivation you would have to seek the face of God to change your heart and life.

Portions of the book of Ezra were written in Aramaic. Our study verse falls under the portion that was in Hebrew. However, the word for *mourn* used in Ezra 10:6 is identical to the word in the Chaldean or Aramaic, with a slight variation in definition. The word is *'abal,* which means to mourn or grieve but in the sense of lacking the feeling of wholeness or completeness. It is mourning over the loss of a loved one or the loss of a relationship that leaves you feeling incomplete. It is the grief that young wife felt for her wayward husband. She felt incomplete and lonely because of the drugs that separated them. That sense of incompleteness and longing to feel joined with her husband created this sense of grief, and she was mourning this loss.

Upon examination of the word for *mourn* in Ezra 10:6 in the LXX, we learn that the Greek word used to translate it comes from *pentheō*. This word means to lament and bewail; very often, it specifically expresses deep sadness over a person's condition. Someone's state is so poor and miserly that it has caused the mourner's heart to break. This isn't walking a lonely street with your head down in a state of melancholy, kicking a can around. It's gut-wrenching sadness.

This brings us to 1 Corinthians 5:1–2. There is immorality in the church at Corinth. In fact, the immorality is so explicit that even the pagans in their culture were sickened by it. What made it even worse was that the Corinthian church was tolerating it! To this, Paul says, *"Ought you not rather to mourn?"* We could translate this as, "Shouldn't your heart be broken over this?" Or "Shouldn't your soul be vexed" or "How come instead you don't have deep, inward anguish" about this? Paul was suggesting that the community's disposition and inward anguish about this matter was the first step to getting things back to proper order in their church.

Let's now return to Ezra 10:6. The word for "mourn" is in a Hithpael form and is a participle. The Hithpael is reflexive so it would be rendered as, "He *caused himself* to mourn." As a participle, we would put this in a present tense as, *"He was causing himself to mourn."* We learn from this that we can make a decision to mourn over sin. Unlike the Corinthians, who just went along with it, we can oppose and protest it, affecting our lives and the lives of those we know with our inner anguish and genuine heartfelt sorrow that we bring to God in prayer.

The young wife did not have to mourn for her husband. She could have lost all love for him and walked away. However, she chose to love her husband, despite his behavior; she chose to stay with him, pray for him, and plead before the throne of God for his soul's salvation. As a result, he gave his life to Jesus, who removed his transgression from her midst.

This is such an important lesson for Christians today. We can choose to mourn. We can choose to keep loving even when there is no reason to love, it is not being returned, or it's being abused. If we make the decision to continue to love, we will mourn and grieve over the loss of this relationship even to the point of being consumed by our grief. When the one causing the grief sees how we continue to love and grieve over them, it will *"heap coals of fire"* on their head (Romans 12:20 KJV). The Holy Spirit will use that to convict them to plead with God to change their hearts.

We live in a day of instant gratification—fast foods, instant entertainment, pills to bring instant relief. Yet some things in life are never meant to come quickly. We need to learn perseverance when it comes to those we love, when it comes to our brothers and sisters in the church. Like the Corinthian church and Ezra, we need to *cause* ourselves to mourn over their transgressions.

Anguish and sorrow over sin is a powerful tool. The change you are looking for in your life may not come until your heart breaks over your present state. This reminds Chris of his friend Jennifer, who he met at a service where he was the guest speaker. She says, "I was a different person back then. I went to the club after!" She met her husband—a good, godly man—not long after that service. She had grown tired of her way of living. She went home one night after partying and was heartbroken about the whole entire *party scene* and her involvement with it. Out of despair and anguish, she told the Lord she wanted nothing more to do with it. Well, the Lord heard her prayer. A week later, Geoff saw her biking, waved at her, and chased her down, smitten by her beauty. They are married with three kids who all honor and fear the Lord. "It happened so fast," Jennifer says. "As soon as I got tired of my sin and grew sad over it, the Lord gave me what I needed."

Perhaps you need to grieve over your sin a bit, or perhaps you need to grieve over the sin of someone you know and love. You might be surprised at how that can change circumstances, you, and other people.

Pray this from your heart:

May my heart rend at the presence of sin and may my anguish turn to joy when sin turns to repentance, oh Lord.

11

HIS PRESENCE SATIATES THE WEARY

For I have ***satiated*** *the* ***weary*** *soul, and I have replenished every sorrowful soul.*
—Jeremiah 31:25 (KJV)

Sometimes, exhausted with toil and endeavor, I wish I could sleep
for ever and ever; but then this reflection my longing allays:
I shall be doing it one of these days.
—Piet Hein

Do you ever feel like your soul is healing? For centuries, theologians have tried to explain the difference between the soul and the spirit. One school of theology says man is made up of three parts: body, soul, and spirit, with soul being our heart or mind. Another school of theology says man has only two parts, body and soul, with soul being the same as spirit. Whatever you believe, most people will admit that there is something inside of them that grows weary.

Jeremiah 31:25 confirms this.

Whatever our soul is, God promises to *satiate* and *replenish* it. The Hebrew word translated as *satiate* is *ravah,* which means "to be intoxicated." It also means "to be drunk," "to be saturated with water," or "to take a bath." In our modern Western society, water is plentiful. We have no concept of what it means to ration water or wonder if we will have enough water to survive. In ancient times, this was a constant concern, so many wars were fought over water rights. David went to a stream to pick up five smooth stones to fight Goliath. (See 1 Samuel 17:40.) That little war was likely being fought over that very stream of water.

In ancient times in the Middle East, the average person rarely took a bath. Even in medieval times, that knight in shining armor rarely took a bath. After wearing that outfit in the hot sun…well, it's no wonder they had to arrange marriages.

In the Jewish community, people only took a bath for religious purposes. The Greeks and Romans established bathhouses for the elite; the common folk were left to their stench. Which brings us to an understanding of what *ravah* or *satiate* really means. If you've ever taken a bath or shower after having been out camping or participating in some athletic event, you know how good it feels to have that water cleansing you of all that sweat and filth. That refreshing feeling is *ravah.* When your soul is weary with sin, discouragement, or failure, God will make you feel like you have just taken a long shower, and your soul, whatever it may be, will feel *ravah.*

Furthermore, in Jeremiah 31:25, the Hebrew word for *weary* is *ayeph,* which has the idea of weariness and also carries the idea of a heavy weight. Hebrew is a picturesque language. Many times, to understand a word in Hebrew, one needs to draw a picture. Here the picture would be leather straps that have become so dried out that they are no longer flexible. Those straps are brittle, cracked, and likely to break. However, if you *ravah* or saturate the leather straps with water, they will once again become strong and flexible.

The ideas behind these words become even more interesting in the LXX. The word *ravah* (*satiate*) gets translated into a Greek word that comes from *methyō*. By definition, it means "to drink freely," "to give drink abundantly," and even "to water thoroughly." In the New Testament, this word is used in John 2:10. Jesus is at a wedding feast at Cana in Galilee, and He turns water into wine because the wine had run out. The wine must have been top shelf because when the master of the feast tastes it, he says, *"Everyone serves the good wine first, and when people have drunk freely* [*methyō*], *then the poor wine. But you have kept the good wine until now."* The master of the feast is explaining how people enjoy wine at weddings. They drink until they are happy and full of delight. For the sake of our study, we can simply observe from this how wine turns the disposition of the one drinking from somber to smiling, from despondency to delight. In the same way that wine lifts the mood, so God satiates our soul. Paul alludes to this in Ephesians 5:18–19:

> *And do not get drunk with wine, for that is debauchery, but be filled with the Spirit, addressing one another in psalms and hymns and spiritual songs, singing and making melody to the Lord with your heart.*

Where this gets quite vivid is looking at the word *'ayeph* (*weary*) in the LXX. The Greek word comes from *dipsaō* and simply means "to be thirsty" and "to have a strong desire for drink." This word is used in 1 Corinthians 4:11 to describe the suffering state of the apostles, who often dealt with almost insurmountable circumstances, such as hunger and thirst, as they preached the gospel. Picture a panting, dehydrated missionary walking through the parched Judean desert, tormented with such thirst that his mouth is wide open as he begs the sky for a few drops of rain. If a miracle happened and it were to suddenly start pouring buckets, the rainfall would *methyō* or thoroughly water the tormented man's thirst while he freely drinks the rain. If you can't imagine his elation, you've never known the despair of thirst.

We're given a couple ways to picture a weary soul who is filled with mental depression or anguish. The first is like dried out, brittle, cracking, and breaking old leather straps. The second is like a parched, panting desert wanderer. These two pictures suggest to us that when God saturates the soul with the refreshing presence of the Holy Spirit, that soul is renewed and again becomes strong and able to endure the emotional distresses of life. No medicine, substance, or stimulant can do for the human soul what the presence of God can do for it. We can imagine Jesus alludes to this when He tells the woman at the well, *"but whoever drinks of the water that I will give him will never be thirsty again"* (John 4:14).

Reportedly, on average, 75 percent of Americans are dehydrated at any given time. That means the majority of us walking around could all use a drink from the garden hose. How many of us have parched souls in need of the living water that comes from being in the presence of our Creator? We do well to make room in our day-to-day lives for God's presence. Wait on Him. Be around those who are full of Him. Pray in the Spirit. Read His Word. Don't show up late to church and miss the precious times of worship. Bring your traumas to speech when you are before Him.

Small things like this will renew the strength of your soul, making it strong and flexible. They may seem inconsequential. However, they are no less inconsequential than a glass of water is to a man crawling through the parched Mojave Desert.

Pray this from your heart:

Your presence, oh Lord, is water to my parched soul. May I freely drink. Every brittle area of my life will be made strong, and it will flourish.

12

THE FOOL SAYS THERE IS NO GOD

*The **fool** says in his heart, "There is no God." They are corrupt, they do abominable deeds; there is none who does good.*
—Psalm 14:1

Chaim was reading something on the Internet that sort of blew him away. In fact, he did some research and was amazed to discover how many reputable scientists, physicists, philosophers, and scholars not only actually believe this, but are using government money to research it. It's not some conspiracy theory held by some fringe group street philosopher; it's a theory that recognized, published, serious scholars believe—people like Nick Bostrom of the University of Oxford; Leonard Susskind of Stanford University; and Sylvester James Gates Jr., a theoretical physicist.

These scholars are trying to find some deep anomaly that would prove we are living in a computer simulation created by some programmer or programming team. They believe that our universe is just a program, and we are living in a simulated reality that comes from a series of 10101010. In fact, Gates alleges he has reached deep into the very core of the atomic structure and found a set of equations that is exactly like the equations that drive search engines and browsers. He claims to have found a computer code written into the very fabric of our cosmos, bits of 1010101. It does not *resemble* computer code but is *actual* computer code.

This was even the subject of the prestigious 2016 Isaac Asimov Memorial Debate[3] conducted by Neil deGrasse Tyson, director of the Hayden Planetarium and a world-renowned astronomer (and atheist). The gist of the theory is that our universe is just a computer simulation like a computer game only much more elaborate, one in which the characters (us) have consciousness. In the *Star Trek* television shows that came out after the original series, the crew members get to relax in a hologram room, where they can enjoy any environment they want. They can go to ancient Egypt or twentieth-century earth and actually interact with the people created by this computer program. These creations have consciousness and intelligence and are able to converse, create, and invent.

Crazy, no? The thing is, all of these scientists and philosophers are atheists; they do not believe in God. As they dig deep into the very fabric of our existence, they cannot deny that there is a greater intelligence at work, but rather than call that intelligence *God,* they have come up with a theory that some computer geek from some other dimension with higher intelligence is playing with his computer. He can just shut down his computer one day, hit the delete button, and make us all vanish from existence. On the other hand, many of these scientists are working to create the same type of simulation so they can create their own virtual world of characters with consciousness and intelligence, so they can become like the Most High and create or destroy at will. We have to wonder why brilliant individuals are willing to believe in a teenage, alien computer geek with godlike qualities yet refuse to accept the existence of a God of the universe.

In Psalm 14:1, perhaps David was prophesying about these scientists who deny the existence of God yet are willing to believe in an

3. "2016 Isaac Asimov Memorial Debate: Is the Universe a Simulation?", www.youtube.com/watch?v=wgSZA3NPpBs.

all-powerful programmer who created them. A scientist only believes what he can prove and see. He cannot prove the existence of God but he feels he can prove and see the existence of a programmer. The Hebrew word for *fool* is *nabel*. There was actually a person named Nabel during David's time, and some commentators believe David was referring to him. Most, however, believe it to be just a play on words, and the word should not be taken as a proper name but for what it means. This is really the proper Semitic approach, and hence it is properly translated as *fool*. This word *nabel* in the original ancient Hebrew was spelled without vowels; these were only added in AD 700. You could easily pronounce the word as "noble." Indeed, that is the meaning of the word, to be "noble and distinguished and yet senseless." It is also the word for *clouds* or *fog*. You see them but there is no substance to them. They are but a vapor that vanishes. You can fly into a cloud or walk through fog and easily lose your way. You do not know what direction you are heading. So it is with these atheistic scientists who refuse to believe in God but cannot deny the existence of some greater power, so they come up with their own idea of a programmer. If they can prove their theory, then you don't need faith to believe in a higher power.

In the LXX, the word *nabel* gets translated into the Greek word *aphrōn*. This is one of those words that has an alpha privative in front of it to negate what comes after. The alpha comes in front of *phren*, which originally meant *diaphragm*, once regarded as the center of intellectual and spiritual ability. The word later lost the physical sense (*diaphragm*) but kept the meaning of "intellectual ability." So *aphrōn* means someone without intellectual understanding. Not to say they don't have intellectual capacity but that they are more deficient of reflection or without proper sense.

Jesus uses a form of this word in Mark 7:21–22, listing things that defile a person. At the end of this list is "*foolishness.*" This is lack of moral reflection. Those who don't believe in an eternal moral Judge will live their lives as though He does not exist. This attitude breeds the sins of immorality listed in these verses. Now you can see why Jesus calls *foolishness* or "lack of moral reflection"—which is often owed to denying there is a God—evil.

Chris remembers listening to an apologist who raised an excellent point. He described a conversation he had with several scientists about the existence of God. Trying to find common ground, he said, "Would you be open to the idea of God's existence if we began with the premise that, if God existed, He isn't interested in humanity's morality? He doesn't care about what choices humans make. He's not trying to tell us what to do and what not to do in the bedroom. He doesn't care who you vote for. He's not interested in the abortion debate. He's not looking over our shoulders, telling what is and isn't a good time. He's a Creator and not a moral lawgiver nor a judge of morality." He said these scientists were more open to the idea of God after that. It seems that their problem with God was not that He is a Creator, but that He is a *moral* Creator.

Perhaps that is why the fool would much prefer an eternal computer programmer, coding us with 101010, instead of a God who is interested in the way we live our lives unto Him. Jesus tells us this attitude is evil and is at the heart of humankind's folly.

In the battle of ideologies, we need to determine what is wise and what is foolish in order to determine who we take our cues from. We can take it from the timeless testament of Scripture that if someone denies the Creator and His moral law, this person is a *nabel* and an *aphron*—a fool. They may appear to be distinguished, yet they are senseless and empty. Their ideas lead to moral breakdown and defilement, both for them and those who listen to them.

Pray this from your heart:

Wisdom begins with the premise that You exist, oh God of my creation and moral judge. I live my life in reverence of Your ways for life is Your design, which I honor with obedience.

13

CLING TO GOD

*Therefore a man will leave his father and his mother and **cling** to his wife, and they will become one flesh.*

—Genesis 2:24 (ISV)

*But all of you who are **clinging** to the LORD your God are alive today.*

—Deuteronomy 4:4 (ISV)

The word *cling* gives us the impression of hanging on for dear life. You cling to a life jacket, you cling to a rock on a ledge, and you cling to your seat in the car if the driver is going too fast. The idea of a man clinging to his wife somehow does not create the picture we think God intended.

Practically every modern English translation uses a different word for the Hebrew word *deveq* or *cling.* What is interesting is that the same word is used for how we are to relate to God: we are to cling to Him like a man clings to his wife.

How can we cling to God, and what does it mean to cling to your wife?

The problem lies in our understanding of the Hebrew word *deveqim,* which comes from the root word *deveq.* You see, we really cannot find a decent English word to use for *deveqim;* it is a word that has to be explained rather than translated. The closest we can come is the word *cling,* meaning "hold fast," "be faithful," "remain faithful," "be loyal" or "adhere." Yet none of these come close to properly giving us an understanding of *deveqim.* It just can't be done adequately with one English word; unfortunately, when translating the Bible, you have to come up with one or maybe two words at the most because there just is not enough space to explain it.

So Chaim goes to his Jewish sources and finds that *deveq* has a very sacred meaning. To modern Jews, *deveq* is an attachment to God, having God always on their minds. It refers to a deep, meditative state attained through prayer and Bible study. In modern Hebrew, *deveq* is the word for *glue.* It is also a synonym in modern Hebrew for dedication toward a particular goal. Yet in religious Judaism, it means attaching yourself to God in all areas of your life. In the state of *deveq,* one hears the voice of God, receives direction from God, and lives in the presence of God. It is unifying all aspects of one's life—body, soul, and mind—with the heart of God.

What is curious is that the word *deveq* is used in Deuteronomy 4:4 as an adjective to modify the noun YHWH, which is prefixed with a definite article. In Hebrew, adjectives function like adjectives in English—they modify, characterize, classify, or describe nouns. This creates real difficulty in translation. If we render *deveq* as *cling,* then as an adjective, it would be *clingy.* This would suggest that we are created and designed to cling to God. We were created for God and to complement God. We were created to fill a hole in God's heart, so to speak. He was the plug that fills that hole. Perhaps it would be better understood if we say we are God's hugger.

Now pause and put all that in light of what a man is to do when he *deveq* or *clings* to his wife. That is much more than just hanging onto her. She is the role model for the relationship we are to have with God. If a man cannot *deveq* or *cling* to his wife, then odds are he will have trouble *deveq*(ing) with God.

There seems to be just one English word that would fit the role for *deveq* and that is *hug. Deveq* is to give God a deep, loving hug every chance you get, just as a man should give his wife a hug every chance he can get when they're alone. Do you ever pray and meditate on God, having a quiet time with Him, when suddenly you feel His presence? That is God giving you a *deveq*, a hug. He designed you and created you to be His. When He cleanses all your sins and makes you a pure and clean vessel, He is free to fulfill His heart's desire, and that is to reach out and give you a hug.

When we go to the LXX, we make an interesting discovery. In Genesis 2:24, the Greek word for *cling* is *proskallaō*. It means "to unite," "to cause two things to stick together," and "to glue." The idea is that two things are brought together quite intensely. In the New Testament, a form of this word, *kollaō*, is used abundantly. *Kollaō* carries much of the same idea: "to glue," "to cement," and "to stick." In antiquity, this was used in one instance to describe the infusing of elements to make a crown.

Chris is fascinated by a guy he follows on social media who does metalworking in his backyard. He tosses copper pennies, aluminum cans, and all kinds of scrap metal into his kiln to make various alloys. It's fascinating to see these elements become joined. There is no undoing what he's done. The bond literally makes the elements one. It's like combining ingredients in a recipe—good luck separating them.

This reminds Chris of the time he was making pancakes at a friend's house. To do something fun, a few friends get together and have breakfast for dinner. Chris was making banana pancakes and had poured the smashed bananas into the pancake mix. His friend's four-year-old daughter came up, her eyes big and curious, and she said, "Can you please take the bananas out? I don't like banana." Chris's heart sunk. How could he say no to such innocence? But the batter was already *kollaō*! So he just made another batch with her favorite: chocolate chips. (No surprise there.)

This is the idea behind the strongest uses of *kollaō*. *Kollaō* is used by Paul to describe being joined to the Lord (1 Corinthians 6:17), and it is used in Matthew 19:5 when Jesus actually quotes Genesis 2:24 as He discusses a man clinging to his wife. In the cases where the New Testament describes a joining to the Lord, or a husband to his wife, we can assume the strongest and most intense meaning of *kollaō*—that is, the tightest of intimacy, a total uniting of two things.

Yet we make another fascinating discovery when we examine the LXX in light of Deuteronomy 4:4. The Greek word for *cling* here is not *proskallaō* or anything related to such. It is *proskeimai*. The idea is that two things live next to one another. As a result, they are absorbed in each other's worlds.

By looking at the combination of what the *kollaō* words mean and combining it with what *proskeimai* means, we start to see further the idea of *cling* in Genesis 2:24 and Deuteronomy 4:4, which goes hand-in-glove with the Hebrew word *deveq*. To cling means to have an intimate union, an inseparable bond, and to be absorbed with each other's world, so that your world is their world and their world is your world.

What better way to illustrate such a bond than with an intimate hug with all the feels. When you cling to the Lord—*deveq, proskallaō/proskeimai*—you become God's hugger. You are joined to Him through your devotion, heart pressed to heart, breath pressed to breath, life pressed to life—like the bond between spouses. It's not just hanging on for dear life in times of trouble. It's a walk of devotion and dedicated interest, day in and day out.

Pray this from your heart:

I am pressed to You, oh Lord, and in You alone are my deepest interests and my most sacred devotion.

14

WHEN GOD HIDES

*And I will surely **hide** my face in that day because of all the evil that they have done, because they have turned to other gods.*
—Deuteronomy 31:18

Chaim ran across something interesting as he was trying to understand why David used three different words for *eternity* in Psalm 119:44. Each word meant eternity, but each had a slightly different nuance. One word for eternity, *'adah,* had a double meaning, both "eternity" and "a prey or spoil." Chaim had read something in Jewish literature years ago about this word but could not remember it. Then the other day, he noticed a little bird on the ground trying to eat a moth. The bird was struggling to *devour* his little prey. After much struggle, he finally *devoured* his dinner, and then turned to look at Chaim and paused as if to say, "You get it?" before flying off. Chaim instantly recalled what he had read about the word *'adah.* It meant more than just a *prey* or a *spoil,* it meant "to struggle with and devour your prey or spoil." The understanding of this word was *hidden* from Chaim but God's little bit of creation was trying to reveal it to him. In modern terms, we would say the answer was hidden in plain sight. Had Chaim not felt that his little feathered friend was jogging his memory and paused to observe this little bit of God's handiwork, he would not have recalled this bit of information about God's Word.

A Jewish scholar named Abraham Heschel often referred to what he called *divine anthropopathy.* We speak of God as anthropomorphic, symbolically ascribing to God a human body, but we rarely consider God anthropomorphically as having humanlike feelings. Heschel told the story of Rabbi Dov Baer, who was walking along a street accompanied by his disciples and saw a little girl hiding in an alcove, weeping. "Why are you crying, little girl?" asked the rabbi. She replied, "I was playing hide-and-seek with my friends, but they didn't come looking for me!" Rabbi Dov Baer sighed and told his students, "In the answer and the tears of that little girl, I heard the weeping of the Shekinah, *'And I will surely hide my face'* (Deuteronomy 31:18)." God is saying that He too has hidden Himself, but no one comes looking for Him. God has hidden Himself in plain sight, but we do not find Him because we are not really looking for Him.

In ancient times, a king would not weep in front of his subjects. He would turn away or hide himself so he could weep in private and not show his emotions. So too in Deuteronomy 31:18. God is not hiding His face so as to punish His people for their evils; He is hiding His face because their evil has cause Him such grief that He must turn away to weep. Their evil was turning to other gods. God had hidden Himself in plain sight, but He was not good enough for them, so they committed spiritual adultery and gave themselves to other gods to meet their needs. Like a rejected lover, God suffered such hurt that He wept, alone and in silence.

If you look at Deuteronomy 31:18 in the Hebrew, you will find the word *hide* is repeated twice. Actually, the first time, the word *hide* is written as an infinitive. In Hebrew, one way to communicate intensity of a verb is to precede it with its own infinitive. Thus, our English translations will render this as "surely hide." But a literal reading of this really speaks of *twice hiding.*

Certain sages suggest that this means that the hiding is itself hidden. God is hidden in His hiding. In the first hiding, God has hidden Himself like the little girl playing hide-and-seek. When we miss His presence, we will come searching for Him. As David said in Psalm 30:7, *"You hid your face; I was dismayed."*

As a college student, Chaim was a reader for a student who had been blind since he was six years old. One evening, he told Chaim, "I have not seen the moon in twenty years." Chaim remembers walking outside, looking up at the moon, and thinking, "You know, you get used to the moon."

So too, we get used to the light of God and His presence, but when we have to go without it, we realize just how important it is. Like David, we are dismayed and will desperately seek to find God. The little girl playing hide-and-seek anticipated the joy of being found by her friends. But when they did not seek her, she remained hidden in her hiding so she could weep over their rejection. So too, if God removes His presence from us and we do not search for Him, this rejection will cause such grief to God that He will hide in His hiding so He may weep.

The word *hide* in Hebrew is *satham,* which means "to conceal" or "to keep secret." It also means "to protect." When you have shared the secrets of your heart with someone, and they betray you, you withdraw from that person and hide the rest of your heart from that person. So it is with God. He will freely share the secrets of His heart with those who love Him, but if we betray Him and seek other gods, He will not only hide His presence from us but He will hide His heart from us as well. He will be hidden in his hiding.

If we look in the LXX, we discover that the word used to translate *satham* is *apostrephō*. This word has a wide range of meanings, including "to turn," "to retreat," "to turn away," and "to hide oneself." It is often used in a negative sense in the New Testament. One example is found in 2 Timothy, where the apostle Paul is anguished because his ministry friends had neglected him in the providence of Asia. He says, *"You know that everyone in Asia has abandoned me, including Phygelus and Hermogenes"* (2 Timothy 1:15 ISV). *Abandoned* is an accurate word to use. Paul is out there doing the work of the ministry, and his friends left him high and dry. They ignored Paul's efforts. They had *apostrephō*…

stranded him and left him in the lurch. He's like the little girl whose friends didn't bother to look for her.

This reminds Chris of the time he was in living California and went out to dinner with friends. They agreed to meet at a restaurant, but when they arrived, they discovered it was closed for remodeling. So Chris hopped in their car, and they went to another pizza place a mile down the road. They talked and ate for a few hours. Before they left, Chris stopped in the restroom. When he came out, his friends were gone. They had forgotten Chris's car was at the restaurant down the street! He called them up, thinking they would come back to pick him up, but instead they said, "It's a warm and beautiful evening. It will just be easier if you walk." Some friends, huh? It wasn't the walk that saddened Chris; it was his friends' neglect. They deserted him and didn't care. An hour ago, they were eating pizza and laughing like pals. Now, Chris was kicking rocks under the stars.

If we are made in God's image, wouldn't He feel the same pain we feel when someone draws away from us? In His grief, as we learn in Deuteronomy 31:18, He will hide His face or presence from us. If we are like David, we will be dismayed and turn around to seek Him again. But if we do not do so, He will *"surely hide"* or hide His hiddenness so that He may weep over His broken heart.

If you no longer feel God's presence, you must first determine if He is just hidden so as to draw you to search for Him, or is He hiding in His hiddenness so He may weep over His heart, which has been broken by us? Perhaps He is hidden in plain sight, and you are just too busy or too proud to think that God will reveal Himself in His creation, even if it is just a humble little feathered creature. God is speaking to us all the time. His voice is all around us in His creation. We are often just too self-absorbed or too busy to pause and listen.

Pray this from your heart:

Lord, turn to me as I turn myself toward You. I acknowledge my transgressions and I sorrow after Your weeping.

15

MURMURING CAUSES IRREPARABLE HARM

*And the people **murmured** against Moses, saying,*
What shall we drink?
—Exodus 15:24 (KJV)

We live in an age where complaining is kind of the thing to do. Yelp, Trip Advisor, Google Review…it's so convenient to hop on and tell the world about the cold french fries they served you at the steakhouse, or the noisy air conditioner in your hotel room. All it takes is one complaint for you to find another option to fit your plans. Dozens of times, Chaim has allowed one reviewer's nightmarish gripe to deter him from making reservations. That's why he tries to take a pause when he has a bad experience before going on Trip Advisor and attempting to ruin someone's business and livelihood.

Just the other day, he was in Boston. He had made reservations for a hotel that had some pretty solid reviews. Chaim specified just what he wanted ahead of time, which the hotel staff seemed pleased to accommodate. But his experience quickly soured the moment he got to the room. First, there was an adjoining door, which is basically like sharing a room with a stranger. And these strangers were making lots of noise. Next, it was clear that the recliner that belonged in the corner of the room was missing. Where the heck did it go? Third, there was no art on the walls. What kind of room was this anyway? This was supposed to be a *nice* hotel.

Marching up and down that hideous room, Chaim pulled up Trip Advisor on his phone and started smashing the buttons. He entitled his review, "This Hotel Blows," and came up with a sob story that made him sound like he had been treacherously victimized. When his crazed fit of hacking and hewing was over, he felt a little better, but that didn't solve the problem. He went to see the manager, who saw that Chaim was obviously in despair. The manager said, "My sincerest apologies. We shouldn't have given you that room. We have upgraded you to a nice suite." Suddenly, Chaim felt embarrassed. The hotel didn't deserve his sinister complaints and malevolent murmuring.

Chaim could sense the Holy Spirit shaking His head, so he removed the review. He repented for not only putting it up in the first place but for only being willing to take it down when he had gotten what he wanted.

The point is, murmuring and trashing people can cause a lot of harm, sometimes even irreparable harm. We see this in the Old Testament in Exodus 15:24 (KJV): *"And the people murmured against Moses, saying, What shall we drink?"*

Some translations say the people or Pharisees *complained* or *grumbled*. In our modern lingo, we would say they were bellyaching. The word used in the Hebrew is *lavan. Lavan* has the idea of demanding a remedy for an undesirable or unfair situation. It is whispering, backbiting, or talking behind someone's back.

When we go to the LXX, we discover something particularly interesting. The Greek word used for *complaining* is *diagongyzō*. It means "to express distaste" and "to show dissatisfaction for disappointed hopes." It is a personal attitude of contempt that causes someone to groan and gossip about the one whom they feel has done them wrong. The New Testament takes advantage of this idea in Luke 5:30. It says, *"And the Pharisees and their scribes grumbled at his disciples, saying, 'Why do you eat and drink with tax collectors and sinners?'"* The word for *grumble* here comes from *gongyzō*. It comes from the same word family as *diagongyzō* and suggests that the scribes and Pharisees were complaining or grumbling over the behavior of Jesus. This included gossiping and slandering Jesus. Luke has purposely used this word to describe the Pharisees' behavior so that the reader might recall the action of the Israelites in the wilderness. In murmuring about Jesus, the Pharisees were repeating the ways of their ancestors. It confirms their rebellious ways. They thought they were pious toward God, but how wrong they were! In their supposed piousness, they couldn't even see that God was in their midst, and they opposed Him through their gossip and criticism.

It is interesting that the text in Exodus tells us first that the people murmured or grumbled against Moses. The problem was not lack of water; Scripture does not say they were thirsty. What we learn from Exodus 15:22–24 is that after crossing the Red Sea, they spent three days in Shur, where they found no water, so they moved on to a place called Marah, which means *bitter* because the water they found was bitter or not suitable to drink. They most likely had a supply of water. This is exactly what the scribes and Pharisees did against Jesus—they talked behind His back, gossiping and trying to destroy His reputation.

The Talmud teaches that destroying another person's name through slander is akin to murder; like murder, the damage is irrevocable. There is an old rabbinical story about a man who went through a community spreading lies about a rabbi. He eventually regretted his gossip and asked the rabbi to forgive him, saying he would do whatever it took to make amends. The rabbi told him to take several feather pillows and scatter the feathers to the wind. The man did this and returned to the rabbi. The rabbi then instructed him to gather all of the feathers. The man said this was impossible. The rabbi replied, "Of course, even though you regret the evil you did and wanted to correct it, as it is impossible to gather all the feathers, so it is to repair the damage done by your words."

The people of Israel were most likely rationing water at this time. Although they had not yet run out of water, they were likely thinking and saying to one another, "Hey, I'm running low on water and that crazy Moses makes us camp for three days at a place where there is no water and now brings us to a place where the water is not drinkable. What's with this guy anyway? Some leader he turns out to be, bringing us out here to the desert to die of thirst. He probably has all the water he needs in his tent; why should he care about us?" They were complaining about Moses's leadership and his behavior just as the scribes and Pharisees complained about Jesus's behavior and the example He was setting as a master teacher.

We have the same problem today in many of our churches where people *lavan* or *gongyzō*. They say, "Hey, that pastor of ours never feeds us with the meat of the Word of God; all we get is milk. He does not bring the Holy Spirit to refresh us with God's presence. What's up with our pastor anyway? What kind of leader is he?" Just the mere *lavan/gongyzō,* whispering your dissatisfaction with someone in leadership, will undermine that leadership, and it could result in the loss of all the good that the leader could accomplish.

God placed this sin of *lavan/gongyzō,* murmuring and complaining, on a very high level of seriousness. For the words spoken in slander, the damage to one's name is irrevocable. By simply complaining that they had no water and blaming Moses for this, the people of Israel undermined his leadership role. Had they succeeded in completely destroying Moses's leadership, they would have been lost and left to die in the desert.

Your gossip, murmuring, or complaining, your *lavan/gongyzō* with your pastor or Christian leader, could result in the loss of a lot of good words that could change your life.

Don't be like the Israelites, the Pharisees, or Chaim when he vented on Trip Advisor. Trashing people, businesses, and churches with your murmuring might cost someone more than you realize. Are you sure you want to scatter those feathers?

Pray this from your heart:

Guard my mouth from murmuring, oh Lord. May my words bring life, not destruction.

16

BROKENHEARTED AND CRUSHED

The Lord *is* ***nigh*** *unto them that are of a* ***broken*** *heart; and saveth such as be of a* ***contrite*** *spirit.*

—Psalm 34:18 (KJV)

The occasion for Psalm 34, as we learn in the first verse, is when David is fleeing from King Saul and seeks refuge with King Abimelech of Gath. This is where he pretends to be insane. (See 1 Samuel 21:10–15.) Most commentators say the Lord being nigh or close to the brokenhearted in Psalm 34 is a reference to being sorrowful over your sins. The remainder of the verse tells us that God saves those of a contrite spirit or one who is afflicted with feelings of guilt. Jewish scholars such as Rabbi Samson Hirsch, a nineteenth-century linguist and Hebrew master, sees this word *dakka'* as more than just merely feeling contrite. Hirsch expresses *dakka'* as being crushed by this burden of guilt. Therefore, a person who is brokenhearted over his sin has a humble spirit and this is the type of person whom God will save.

The word *broken* for brokenhearted is *lenishebere* from the Hebrew root word *shava*. This word is in a Niphal participle form. The word *shavar* means "to be shattered into splinters." It is a word used by workers in a quarry who chip away at rocks to make them fit the project the stones will be used for. As a Niphal particle, it would read that God is near to those whose heart is being chipped away. As a Niphal, it would have a reflexive nature to it, indicating that the brokenhearted person is chipping away at his or her heart. We have the English idiom "eat your heart out," which expresses the idea of gradually being consumed by grief and bitterness. We're sure that as David fled from Saul, he probably spent a lot of time trying to figure out what went wrong and what he might have done that would have made Saul so hateful toward him. The more David thought about it, the more he was consumed by grief and guilt or *shavar*.

However, the whole context of Psalm 34 seems to have nothing to do with sin and redemption, at least in reference to David. If we stop to consider David's plight, we will see a different context. David trusted and honored King Saul, yet in a fit of jealousy and anger, Saul tried to kill David. Imagine how you would feel. One day, you are a national hero, and the next, you are fleeing for your life with a price on your head.

The average person would feel betrayed, dejected, and heartbroken. They would also feel really humbled to have reached a point where they would have to pretend to be insane just to save their life.

When we turn to the LXX, we will discover that the Greek word used to translate *dakka'* is *tapeinos*, which means "to be lowly" or "to be insignificant." It refers to a servant who is obedient to his or her master due to their lowly social status, having an essentially submissive disposition. The servant does what he is told. There's no fight in him. He gives no pushback. This word is used in 2 Corinthians 7:6 when Paul says, *"But God, who comforts the downcast, comforted us by the coming of Titus."* Paul had been through a crisis with his church in Corinth, and the situation beat him down. The ministry had taken its toll on the apostle. Life was kicking him in the teeth.

When you have been through enough of life, it sure does take the life out of you, doesn't it? This is when you can lose your drive.

This is especially true in ministry. How often do pastors and leaders get crushed as they serve the Lord and lose what it takes to go on? So often, like David, they will blame themselves and become deeply introspective about what more they could have done. It's a slow death. Eventually they just get to the place where they, like a servant, will just take what they are given.

Yet Paul also does something interesting by using the word *tapeinos*. He is alluding to Isaiah 49:13 wherein the prophet says, *"For the LORD has comforted his people and will have compassion on his afflicted* (*tapeinos*)." Paul is noting that the fight isn't over for God's servants who've been crushed. When the servants of the Lord have lost their will to go on, the Lord gives them strength.

How does God do this? Psalm 34:18 (KJV) tells us, *"The LORD is nigh unto them that are of a broken heart."*

The Hebrew word for *nigh* is *qarav*, which means to be near in the sense of being a relative. God is a relative to the brokenhearted. But *qarav* is also the word for a scorpion. Scorpions have a bad reputation as being venomous with a painful often fatal sting. Actually, of the 2,000 known species of scorpions, only twenty-five are known to have a venom that is harmful to humans. Only one species in the United States has a venom that could be harmful and maybe fatal only to a small child, not to adults.

The ancients observed scorpions and were fascinated by their mating rituals. A male and female would grab hold of each other and do a little dance together. Eventually, the male would move the female to a safe, out-of-the-way site to consummate their relationship. It might be this intimacy that David is referring to when he says that God is *qarav* to the brokenhearted. God is a close relative of the brokenhearted, joining them in an intimate little dance. It is interesting that after the mating takes place, the male scorpion quickly dies, and the female scorpion's body is torn apart in giving birth to the young scorpion, killing her and leaving the young scorpion an orphan. There is a sort of death that takes place when love has been betrayed, resulting in a broken heart. It is a death to a relationship. But that death to the relationship not only affects the one whose heart has been broken but also the heart of the heavenly Father. Thus, the one breaking another's heart not only kills the relationship with that person but also kills his relationship with God.

Why does God give such special attention to the brokenhearted? When someone you love has a broken heart, your heart is also broken. But there is another reason God has a close relationship with the brokenhearted. His heart is not only broken for the ones He loves who have suffered a broken heart, but we break His heart daily. He knows better than anyone what a broken heart is like.

The Lord is not only near to the brokenhearted because His heart is broken, but He will save those who have a contrite or *dakka'/tapeinos* spirit that has been crushed, shattered, and splintered, a spirit that's been mauled by life. God will piece it back together and use that shattered spirit to again perform acts that are in harmony with Him. He can use that *dakka'/tapeinos* spirit to draw one closer to Him, to reach out to others who are hurting, to weep with those who weep, and to comfort those who feel orphaned by a betrayal of their love.

Pray this from your heart:

Draw near to me, oh Lord, for my spirit is crushed and broken. Your nearness renews me and gives me the will to go on.

17

GOD GIRDS US WITH STRENGTH

It is God that ***girdeth*** *me with strength,*
and maketh my way perfect.
—Psalm 18:32 (KJV)

There are some things you don't try to be good at in life. The talent is just there. First you notice it and then others notice it without you ever having to mention how talented you are.

Chaim has discovered that he has an innate ability to cook. He decided to hone this raw talent by taking a few cooking classes at the nearby college, led by a five-star Michelin chef. This dude commanded respect. As soon as he entered the room, dressed in his chef's whites, he looked all of students over with a stern look in his eyes that said, "I'm going to teach you novices how to be great like me." To Chaim's surprise, his first lesson wasn't about cuisine, but about how a chef must dress. For a half an hour, this teacher told the students why they had to spend $60 on a chef's coat in order to be part of this class. Before Chaim knew it, he was wearing his own chef's whites—hat, coat, and apron. With newfound confidence, he felt ready to do some battle in that kitchen. He took himself seriously and expected more from himself. He was cooking with the big boys. The chef had girded those students with strength.

God girds us with strength.

The English word *gird* means to encircle with a belt or band. Some translations say that the Lord "arms us" with strength, "clothes us" with strength, or "encircles us" with strength. *Encircles* seems to be the best English word here. The word in Hebrew is *'azar,* which means "to join together" and "to hold together." As a noun, it is used for a belt or girdle.

The *girdle* was an important part of the Eastern dress, sort of like a belt used to draw the garment tightly to the body, particularly while on a journey or doing battle. Here the word is used as a verb, which is in a Piel (intensive) form; as such, it forms a double accusative. That is why there's a definite article, *the,* before the word *God,* to show that both God and strength are the direct objects. It is just not God's strength that is tightly wrapped around us, but it is God Himself that is wrapped around us. As a Piel, it is intensive, which means He is hugging us with His strength. The word *'azar* is used tropically or comparatively for strength to indicate that He has a very strong grip around us.

The Hebrew word *El* is used for God rather than the word *YHWH* for a good reason, according to Jewish scholars. Unlike Christian scholars who explain the different or interchangeable use of the words *Elohim* and *YHWH* for God in biblical criticism as an indication of different authors of the text, Jewish scholars teach that the word *Elohim* is in a masculine form and the word *YHWH* is in a feminine form. *El* or *Elohim* is used to indicate the masculine nature of God, His provision and protection. The word *YHWH* is used to express the feminine nature of God, His mercy, love, and nurturing characteristics. Thus it is *El* or *Elohim* who wraps His arms around us to protect us.

What we discover in the LXX is also fascinating. The translators have used the word *perizōnnymi* to translate *'azar.* This literally means "to dress for action." In antiquity, it was commonly used to describe individuals in their respective trades getting dressed for work, or athletes or warriors dressed for action. For instance, it is used to describe a cook putting on their apron before preparing a meal, an athlete putting on his uniform before a game, or a ballet dancer putting on her leotard and tutu before a performance.

The word *perizōnnymi* is used a number of places in the New Testament but most interestingly in two places. In Luke 12:35, when Jesus talks to His disciples about being ready for His second coming, He says, *"Stay dressed for action* (*perizōnnymi*)." This is an illustration of man who has his robe tucked into his belt and is ready to run, emphasizing vigilance. And in Ephesians 6:14, in which Paul is telling his church to put on the armor of God, he goes through the armor piece by piece and gets to the belt, saying, *"Stand therefore, having fastened on* (*perizōnnymi*) *the belt of truth."* Hitching up the belt was imperative to successful, active service.

In Psalm 18:32, the LXX is teaching us that God prepares us for effective service. Let's face it—life is a battle. We are constantly bombarded with trials, tests, temptations, and the traps of the devil. You name it, and it could be coming our way at a moment's notice. Yet God does not place us out there unprepared. Like a chef who enters the kitchen with his or her apron on or a football player who takes to the field with their helmet, shoulder pads, and cleats, God sends us into battle all girded up, ready for service, with both Himself and His strength.

What is very curious is the Hebrew word used for the word *strength* with which God grips us to protect us. The common word in Hebrew for *strength* is *ozaz,* but in Psalm 18:32, the Hebrew word that is used is *chyil,* which has the idea of twirling or spinning around in a circle and dancing. God is the lead partner in a dance with you. He keeps a tight grip on you, leading you as you dance with Him through your problems and through your life.

People spend a lot of money going to an amusement park or carnival that has numerous rides that do nothing more than spin them around in a circle. There is something very pleasurable about spinning. In ancient times, children often worshipped God by *chyil*—spinning in a circle. Chris once attended a worship service where people were expressing a heartfelt worship with uplifted hands. Suddenly a little child run into the aisle and began to spin around in a circle, just smiling, singing, and twirling out of pure joy.

Chris recalls reading a story about a Christian pastor in a country with a repressive government that imprisoned him for nothing more than being a Christian. This pastor was placed in a solitary prison cell and wrote that his strength was truly *"the joy of the LORD"* (Nehemiah 8:10). God filled him with such joy that he began to dance in that prison cell, worshipping God. The cell was so small that all he could do was *chyil*— dance or twirl around in a circle, singing praise to God out of pure joy. He was not dancing alone. Jesus was right there with him, *'azar* holding him, hugging him, and *chyil* dancing right along with him.

For many of us, the cares of this world so weigh us down that we can only sit and wring our hands in despair. Yet, we don't need to worry and fret. We could be dancing with God, who will lead us around all our problems.

Pray this from your heart:

Gird me with Yourself, oh Lord, and make me ready for action. You lead me in a dance where I find safety and protection.

18

GRACE IS ACCEPTANCE

But Noah found ***grace*** *in the eyes of the* Lord.
—Genesis 6:8 (KJV)

For by ***grace*** *you have been saved through faith. And this is not your own doing; it is the gift of God.*
—Ephesians 2:8

Grace means "unmerited favor." This is pretty basic knowledge for anyone who has been around church for more than a few months. But the Hebrew and Greek words for *grace* illustrate to us some nuances that are quite helpful.

In Genesis 6:8 (KJV), the Hebrew word for *grace* is given in its Semitic root, which is just two letters. It is the word *chen* or Cheth Nun. Chaim believes the Semitic root is used to make a play on the word *Noah,* which is *chen* spelled backward, Nun Cheth or *Noach,* which means *rest.* The root word for *grace* is often given as Cheth Nun Nun, which means *favor.* But Jewish rabbis will challenge this and say the Hebrew triliteral root is Cheth Nun Hei, which means "to encamp" and "to set up tents." Chaim believes the use of the Semitic root indicates that both Hebrew roots were intended to be used.

It is not enough to say Noah found favor in the eyes of God. What does that really mean? How did he find favor in the eyes of God? The word play off of *Noah* tells us he found grace or favor in God by resting in God and doing nothing.

When we examine the word *grace* in the LXX, we discover that Paul uses the Greek word *charis* in Ephesians 2:8 to let the Ephesians in on the fact that our salvation comes by grace, not works: *"For by grace you have been saved through faith. And this is not your own doing; it is the gift of God."* Fittingly, Paul's understanding of *grace* confirms what the word play in the Hebrew tells us: we are saved by just resting in God, doing nothing but applying faith.

Still, that doesn't show us how Noah found this grace. By tracing this word to its very Semitic origin of *chen*, we find it is used for an encampment or pitching tents. In ancient times, encampments were a family thing. There is safety in numbers, so the Bedouin tribes or families would travel in a large group and set up camp. They would pitch their tents in a large circle, setting up a wall surrounding the families. No one was allowed to enter their encampment because they did not trust anyone outside their family. The only way to find refuge in an encampment would be to show you were a member of the family. This traditional way of life—allowing outsiders in only if they become "blood brothers"—has been known throughout the world.

Grace is unmerited favor as God extends to everyone the privilege of becoming a member of His family by being born again through the shed blood of His Son Jesus. Just as a person has to prove himself worthy of becoming a member of a tribe to find rest in that tribe or family, we are born again or become worthy of becoming a member of God's family and finding rest in the safety of His encampment. This is accomplished by simply believing that God's Son shed His blood for us; it is by faith, and it is a gift that we receive for no other reason than God loves us. There is one other definition of *chen* other than grace: *acceptance*.

This makes Chris think of the various times he has been to Sicily, where he has found unparalleled favor. Chris has been to forty-seven nations, many of which he visited to teach the Scriptures, but none have shown him as much favor as the Sicilians. From the moment his plane landed on the coast back in 2013, the people in the churches there were as near and dear to Chris as family. It's been ten years, and he hasn't lost touch with any of them.

His translator, a full-blooded Italian, once told Chris, "I have seen lots of preachers come here but none of them have been so accepted into this culture as you have. It's like you are family." Why? The translator said, "It is your great-grandparents' Italian blood." He said it as a bit of a joke but he was being serious. Chris's great-grandparents were from Palermo; they were full-blooded, tomato-sauce bottling, homemade wine-making Italianos. Chris never got a chance to meet them because they died quite some time before he was born. But they live in him through their blood, which they passed on to him and which has given him tremendous acceptance in the nation of Italy. Chris's Sicilians friends consider him to be a member of their family. He is accepted, and they show him favor. Now that's grace.

In the same way, all of us Christians are accepted into the family of God because of the blood of Jesus Christ. His blood has given us grace and acceptance into His camp.

We are approaching the camp of God and request that we be allowed to enter the safety of that encampment. God simply says, "You have to be My child to enter. You must prove worthy." Then God's Son Jesus steps forward and says, "This child is worthy because I died for this person." Then Jesus turns to you and asks, "Do you want to be a child of God and enter our encampment?"

Now it is up to you, either say yes or no. If you say *yes*, you are allowed the privilege of entering the encampment of God and receiving all the benefits and protection that encampment has to offer. That is what grace is all about.

Pray this from your heart:

I am deeply grateful for Your sacrifice, oh Lord—for Your offer of favor, even grace. I receive this and am humbled to be freely admitted into Your family.

19

THE YOUNG BRIDEGROOM

And as the ***bridegroom*** *rejoices over the* ***bride****,*
so shall your God rejoice over you.
—Isaiah 62:5

Marriage is an important theme that runs through the entire Bible. There's so much that comes with marriage, isn't there? As a result, it can illustrate a surplus of things, including various aspects of our relationship with God.

Let's look at Isaiah 62:5. The Hebrew word for *bridegroom* here is *katan,* which is another word for *marriage*. This word for marriage has the idea of joining together in complete truth and honesty. When God as the bridegroom is married to us, He is joined to us in complete truth.

Okay, that is God's side of the deal; He is the bridegroom. But what are we as the bride or *kallah*? In its Semitic root, the word *kallah* has a double meaning of both destruction and completion. In marriage, your life as a single person is destroyed. It is no longer "my things," but "our things." Yet being joined with another person in marriage is really a completion of the way God designed us. This sort of flies in the face of our modern thinking in which we put ourselves first. As God said, "*Therefore a man shall leave his father and his mother and hold fast to his wife, and they shall become one flesh"* (Genesis 2:24). Looking out for number one involves two people, but hey, we're just the messengers.

Chaim was recently reading in the Zohar and ran across a rather interesting thought. The Jewish sages teach that there are three types of prayer:

- The prayer of a child to a parent: "Oh God, please give me..." That seems to fit the majority of us.
- The more mature prayer of the wife to the husband: "How can I help You and serve You?" There is much more on this but you have probably heard sermons and read books on what it means for us to be the bride of Christ.
- The third way to pray to God is from the standpoint of us as the husband and God as the wife. That may sound a bit creepy but consider: A husband wishes to protect his wife's feelings, her heart. He does not want to offend her or wound her heart. God not only made Himself vulnerable by coming to earth to experience our suffering in the flesh, but He has also made Himself vulnerable by giving us His heart when we give Him ours.

If we give our hearts to someone and that person betrays us, ignores us, does not consider our feelings, or only uses our love to get what they want, they can deeply wound us, hurt us, and break our hearts. God has made Himself just as vulnerable to us; we can deeply wound Him, hurt Him, and break His heart if we just make demands of Him without considering His desires, His pleasure. We can break His heart if we seek other gods to meet our needs and neglect Him.

When we go to the LXX, we discover that the Greek word for *bridegroom* in Isaiah 62:5 is *nymphios*. It is the typical word used in the New Testament to refer to a groom, like in the passage of the wedding feast at Cana. (See John 2:9.) What all the uses of the term *nymphios* have in common in the New Testament is that they describe a man on the day of his wedding. This is why in some lexicons, the word entry includes the definition "young husband" or "newly married husband," emphasizing that this is a new venture the man is undertaking. Any married person understands how challenging the first few years of marriage can often be. The destruction of one's own singular will needs to take place over and over again. If not, neglect of the bride will cause trouble in the marriage.

Chris's married buddies forewarn him that he is going to have to give up some of his particular ways once he weds. One of his friends discovered, to his surprise, that he couldn't go golfing anytime that he wanted to after he tied the knot. Actually, his rather intensive golfing habits, particularly on Saturday mornings, began to hurt his marriage because his wife felt neglected. There he was on the golf course on weekends, putting for birdie, while his wife was left alone doing brunch for one. "Don't make the mistake I made early on in marriage," he told Chris. Citing Chris's travel schedule, he added, "You will have to either take her with you or cut back. But whatever you do, don't neglect her."

This friend learned the hard way that a young groom needs to protect his wife's heart and entreat her to be part of everything he does. He taught the sport to her, and now they're in a golf league together.

As Christians, we need to grow or mature. Do you make God part of everything you do? When you willingly committed to following Jesus, did you consider that He now has to become part of your life? We imagine the last thing any of us would want to do is leave God to poke at His omelet while we are out there playing golf. We cannot leave God in the dust when we are making choices about our life. We need to include Him in the plans. Showing interest here and there is not enough for a healthy, thriving relationship.

Remember, God made Himself vulnerable to us. He paid the ultimate sacrifice for us to have eternal life and live in peace with Him. We owe it to God to consider His heart and the sacrifice He's made to draw near to us. We can do this by imploring Him with consideration in our meditations and prayers, and then by being obedient to Him as the Lord of our life. That's being mature.

Pray this from your heart:

You have made Yourself vulnerable, oh Lord, in giving Yourself as a sacrifice to us. Be near me. I desire Your presence in all I do.

20

THE BEAUTIFUL WILDFLOWERS

*I am a **rose of Sharon**, a **lily** of the valleys.*
—Song of Solomon 2:1

*Consider the **lilies**, how they grow: they neither toil nor spin,*
yet I tell you, even Solomon in all his glory
was not arrayed like one of these.
—Luke 12:27

Many of us grew up hearing Luke 12:27 quoted and were reminded that we need not worry about being clothed because God will take care of that, just as He does for the lilies of the valley. We don't need to worry about what to eat either because if He feeds the birds, He will feed us. Jesus is telling us that our priorities should be in seeking the kingdom of God and not worrying about what we will eat or wear. But we think He is saying much more than that.

Let's consider these *lilies* for a moment. The word *lily* in the Song of Solomon is the Hebrew word *shoshan* from the root word *shush*. In the Aramaic, it is the word *shoshanatha* from the root word *shosh*. Nobody really knows what the Shulamite woman meant when she said she was a *lily* of the valleys. In fact, no one is really sure what a *shush* is; we are guessing that we are talking about a *lily,* a very ornamental flower that *grows wild.*

The Shulamite woman also claims to be a *rose of Sharon*. The word for *rose* in Hebrew is *chabatseleth,* which doesn't mean a *rose* at all. Well, it might. We are not sure. People in those days did not have botanists who categorized all the flowers with some long, unpronounceable names. What we do know for sure is that the *chabatseleth* is a wildflower, possible reddish in color.

What a *chabatseleth* and *shoshan* have in common is that they are *wildflowers*—beautiful, yes, but not beautiful because of some human effort. These flowers are not hybrids, nor are they part of a plan by some human gardener who carefully grew them in a way to accentuate their beauty. They are naturally beautiful. Their Maker has clothed them with everything they need, without their own toil.

When we examine Song of Solomon 2:1 in the LXX, we discover that the Greek word for *lily* is *krinon,* the same word used in Luke 12:27. Like the word *shoshanatha,* it is mainly referring to a *wildflower*. Scholars don't think Jesus really had any particular flower in mind. Most likely, He was referring to the beautiful blooms that dress the landscape all over Galilee. But it could also refer to the cherry blossoms in New York City, the Barbara Karst bougainvillea in Palm Springs, California, or even the Saguaro cacti in Arizona. These are wild blooms that are naturally beautiful, without any human interference.

In Luke 12:27, Jesus is following the same line of thinking found in Song of Solomon 2:1. He's saying that beauty comes from our Maker. Worry, business, and fretting tampers with that. When sinful humans try to create beauty without the Creator in mind, things turn ugly.

But there is another layer of meaning to this, perhaps one we might have missed in Sunday school. Keep in mind that Jesus *is* this Rose of Sharon, and He *is* the Lily of the Valley. He is the wildflower that grows in the field. The point is, He is beautiful without us attempting to put our own spin on Him. In a day and age when branding is everything, we shouldn't feel the pressure to have to *sell* Jesus.

A lot of money was recently spent on an ad campaign to *sell* Jesus on national television. The problem was that it upset both the left and the right! Literally nobody was happy about how Jesus was portrayed, so, ironically, it brought both sides together! The fact is that trying to *sell* Jesus is ugly. Jesus, who represents beauty and peace, doesn't need an ad campaign.

Chris lived for a time in Palm Desert, California. Of all the places he has been to in the USA, this is his favorite. There is desert, mountains, blue sky, and pink flowers everywhere you look. The prime time is in January, when it is a comfortable 75 degrees, the flowers are in bloom, and the mountains have snowcaps. Chris never had to convince anyone that the landscape was beautiful, or tried to sell the thought that the Barbara Karst blooms were lovely.

No one should try to dress Jesus up as hip, cool, and up to date. He doesn't need for us to put our spin on Him; He is beautiful in Himself. Once more He is interested in what the Father created, not what man creates.

Remember this, God is interested in *His* creation and not ours. His creation makes Him smile, not our own. As it applies to us, He is not interested in our good works, our *holy* appearance, or our pious prayers. He is only interested in the real us, not the show we put on for others.

The message in Luke is that there is a natural beauty. In a Jewish wedding, the bridegroom will cover his bride's face with a veil to make a statement. He is saying, "You are beautiful, but that is not why I am marrying you. Beauty will fade as we age but there is an inner beauty that I have fallen in love with that will never fade." God is after the authentic, the real deal.

During Chris's first year at Bible college, one of the school's founders spoke at a chapel service. He was well in his nineties, his voice shook, and he needed support to stand. On top of all of this, he decided to sing a song at the end of his message. It was what the students expected… but then did not expect. Yes, his voice cracked, he was off-key most of the time, and he never took a breath in the right place, but when he finished, there was not a dry eye in the audience. Chris's roommate, who was rather cynical, surprised him when he leaned over and said, "Boy, you know where that song came from." As everyone gave the founder a standing ovation, he did not have to say, "Give it all to God." They knew who was to get the glory, and it was not the elderly founder, but God who shined through him. The founder was truly a lily of the valley and a rose in the field of Sharon.

Pray this from your heart:

You, my God, are the source of all that is beautiful. May I never tamper with that. Rather may I have eyes that recognize what is truly delightful in Your sight.

21

A STEP BACK

Howbeit in the business of the ambassadors of the princes of Babylon, who sent unto [Hezekiah] *to enquire of the wonder that was done in the land, God* **left** *him, to* **try** *him that he might know all that was in his heart.*
—2 Chronicles 32:31 (KJV)

The question that surfaces here is, "What does it mean that God left Hezekiah to try him so He could know all that was in his heart?" Doesn't God know our hearts? Does He really have to leave us to test us so He can know our hearts?

Recently, someone was asking Chaim about this passage of Scripture. He compared notes from the Bible to what archaeology has uncovered about Judah and this time period. Biblically, we know that Hezekiah, the king of Judah, was the son of Ahaz and was a good, godly king. He destroyed all the idolatry he could get his hands on and even destroyed the bronze serpent fashioned by Moses because people had started to worship it. We actually have some archaeological discoveries that might confirm this.

Here's the kicker: despite all these godly acts, Judah went through some of the most trying times to date. Both the Bible and historical records tell us that the Assyrian army, led by their king Sennacherib, invaded both Israel and Judah, took control of the former, and almost succeeded in taking Judah. According to clay tablets written by Sennacherib that are now housed at the Oriental Institute at the University of Chicago, the Assyrian king—a proverbial politician—called his great defeat in Judah a victory, saying he conquered forty-six cities and forced King Hezekiah to pay him tribute. This is all true...but he does not mention that in one night, according to 2 Chronicles 32:21, an angel brought a plague on Sennacherib's army. History tells us they came down with dysentery; 185,000 soldiers died, and Sennacherib was forced to return home in disgrace. Later, two of his sons killed him as he was leaving a pagan temple.

The political climate at this time put Babylon as the trophy for Assyria. Babylon, Judah, and Egypt were having a hard time fighting the neighboring kingdom. Babylon sent envoys to Judah to meet with Hezekiah, supposedly to congratulate him on his great healing and the supernatural deliverance of Jerusalem. (See, respectively, 2 Kings 20:1–15; 2 Kings 19:35.) The Babylonians actually believed God afflicted the Assyrians with dysentery and were intrigued by the miracle of the sundial's shadow going back ten steps, which God sent to confirm that Hezekiah would not die from his illness. (See 2 Kings 20:11.) This greatly interested and impressed the Babylonian astronomers, who watched the skies. As we used to say in the Baptist church, they were "ripe for salvation." Yet the real purpose of these envoys was to encourage Hezekiah to join in an alliance against Assyria. What did this godly king Hezekiah do? He went and showed off all the wealth and military might that Judah had and never once mentioned God in any of this. We're sure this really broke God's heart.

This brings us to our study verse, where we learn that when these ambassadors arrived, God left. God wanted to *try* Hezekiah so He could know his heart. The Hebrew word for *left* is *azavu,* which is in a Qal form. More telling this is in a perfect tense and a passive voice. This means that God had already put Hezekiah's heart to the test. He knew that Hezekiah intended to show off the wealth he had to impress Babylon, and God could not be a part of this great act of disobedience. God had already left, or forsaken him. Yet *forsaken* seems to be a little harsh. Another way to express *azavu* is simply "stepping back" rather than forsaking. It is a simple verb that does not have an intensive inflection. So we could render this as simply God stepping back or removing His presence or influence.

A look into the LXX doesn't seem to disagree with this. The word the translators picked to translate *azayu* is *enkataleipō*. It has a wide range of meanings, including "forsaking," "leaving behind" and "letting go." It can also mean to "let someone remain," or even "let someone exist or be." In Hebrews 10:25, *enkataleipō* is translated as *neglect*. In this passage, the author of Hebrews was exhorting the saints to not let go of church attendance. "Don't leave meeting with one another in the house of the Lord" seems to be the idea.

Leaving church attendance in the dust doesn't always have to be some sort of harsh and intentional protest against showing up. It can be as easy as taking a step back. This seemed to be what a number of formerly churchgoing people did during the COVID-19 pandemic—they just let their church be without making bones about it. They weren't found there, even after the restrictions had lifted. Some told Chris that they didn't have any real intent to forsake church, saying, "I'll be back one day, I am sure." Now, of course, we all do hope they get back into church! The point is, they just took a step back and pulled their presence away from the congregation. Some who were leaders even said, "I just needed to take a step back." Perhaps this is why the author of Hebrews has to rebuke some of the saints. They were stepping back. Drawing away. Giving themselves space. This may be what *azayu* might be suggesting God has done in 2 Chronicles 32:31. He has put a space between Himself and Hezekiah.

Hezekiah was blinded to the fact that his heart was set not upon God but upon *"an arm of flesh"* (2 Chronicles 32:8), even though he himself had reassured his people otherwise. Babylon was the very nation that would take Judah captive in a few years, yet here was Hezekiah leaning in to these people to help him rather than using the great miracles that God performed to encourage these pagan rulers to put their trust in Jehovah. So God rightfully took a step back.

So what about this business of testing or trying God's heart? The word *try* or *test* in Hebrew here is *nasah,* which in its Semitic root has the idea of writing an essay. God was stepping away, giving Hezekiah the opportunity to read God's heart, God's argument.

There is a picture here of a lover who has faithfully given and cared for his beloved only for her to take all of his gifts to adorn herself to impress another lover. God is the forsaken lover, who steps back and lets His unfaithful beloved pursue another lover, hoping that in the process, she will understand how she has broken His heart.

Sometimes, you get used to God. He answers your prayers and provides for you and before long, like Hezekiah, you tend to take Him for granted. When you start to take credit for the wonderful things God does in your life, He needs to step back with His presence. You then begin to realize what you have lost and awaken to the fact that you have broken the heart of the God you love.

That old cliché, "You never know what you had until it's gone," is true. You really don't realize what you've had until you are left alone, on your own, without it. In Hezekiah's case, God had taken a step back, and Hezekiah was found without His presence.

When we act with disobedience, God will withdraw His presence. This is why you hate it when you sin—because you miss God. That hatred for sin is a good thing. It signals that God's heart is grieved, and His stepping back is what draws us back to Him.

Pray this from your heart:

Draw near to me, oh Lord, as I step toward You. For Your presence is what gives me life; may it never withdraw from me.

22

A SUDDEN FALL

*Though he **fall**, he shall not be utterly cast down; for the Lord upholds him with His hand.*
—Psalm 37:24 (NKJV)

Ever have a big fall—one in which you suddenly and unexpectedly trip, time slows down, and you find yourself sitting on your tush? Happens to us all. Perhaps Chaim's most memorable fall came when he was on the island of Malta, teaching at a church there. Some of the people from the church wanted to show Chaim around, so they took him to the Blue Lagoon for an afternoon of beach fun. Blue Lagoon differs from most beach sites in that it is made up of rock, so when you walk around, you could end up slipping on loose gravel if you aren't careful.

Chaim was so busy admiring the sights and enjoying the smell of the surf that he suddenly tripped, fell, and was rolling around in the dirt. He heard a snicker and saw a group of young women from France laughing at him—really laughing. Chaim's hosts were embarrassed for him; they could see he was really struggling.

Chaim likes to think that he's a pretty decent guy. After all, he was there in Malta teaching the Scriptures. But all good men suddenly fall at times—and Psalm 37:24 seems to be suggesting this.

This verse refers to the *"good man"* in verse 23 whose steps are ordered by God. Apparently, as we get to verse 24, we find that this man may eventually fall. The word *though* is *ki* in Hebrew and is most often rendered as "because." This tends to give the idea that a fall is certain. The Hebrew word for *fall* is *napal*. It means "to fall," but it has a variety of usages, such as "falling in battle," "falling wounded," "falling in sickness," or the "falling of one's countenance as in sorrow." The psalmist, King David, seems to be making the point that although we may be walking in steps ordered by God, that does not mean that we will be free of wounds or sorrow. Our road can filled with difficulty.

This brings us to the LXX. The translators chose the Greek word *piptō* to translate the Hebrew word *napal*. This is the common usage of the word in the New Testament. As such, like *napal*, it has a wide range of meanings, including "to collapse," "to fall to pieces," and "to fail." One nuance of this word means that things suddenly get worse—in modern vernacular *things go south*. Like saying, "The stock market went south today," or "The weather on my vacation really went south after the beautiful day we had on Wednesday."

The word *piptō* came to Chris's mind while he was watching a college basketball game during March Madness. A No. 14 seed was up most of the game on a No. 3 seed. It looked like there might be an upset, and Chris walked away from the TV, sure that this one was in the books. But when he returned, things had gone south for the No. 14 seed. Their opponent went on a 9-0 scoring run to eek their way back into the game and win. It happened all so suddenly. The 14 seed began to wobble, fell to pieces, gave up their lead, and then lost.

In the New Testament, James writes, *"My brethren, count it all joy when you* ***fall*** *into various trials, knowing that the testing of your faith produces patience"* (James 1:2–3 NKJV). This introduction deals with the inevitable trials that all believers experience, no matter how close they walk with God. For James's audience, these trials included being treated without dignity, being the recipients of economic discriminations, and even sickness. (See, respectively, James 2:2–4; 5:4; 5:14–16.) The Greek word here for *fall, peripiptō,* comes from *piptō.* It's not going too far to suggest that James is talking about a sudden calamity that tries the faith of a believer. One moment, they are ahead in the game, but no sooner than they can blink, the wheels start to fall off—and things head south, fast.

Here's the sober reality of these two verses: things will ultimately go south at some point, no matter how good they seem now. It could be an injustice that threatens your livelihood and professional career. Maybe it's betrayal. God forbid it's the kind of doctor's report that anyone might shudder to hear. We know this is not a popular thing to say or even an encouraging thing to hear or something you want to read in a devotional that is meant to uplift your faith. We don't want you to worry or withdraw your faith in God. Yet looking at Psalm 37 and James, we discover that it *is* the truth based on the language from the text. Falls are inevitable.

But a sudden fall is not where it ends. James informed his audience that God has made provision for us during these times. (See James 1:3–5.) This is right on par with David, who suggested that when the good man does fall, his support and shelter come from God.

If and when we do fall, we will not be utterly cast down. Our new home is not going to be the dust. When a *good person* whose steps are ordered by God goes through a time of sorrow or is wounded, the Lord will uphold them and lift them up.

Pray this prayer from your heart:

Lord, when things should suddenly fail, You will be there to lift me up. Your hand sustains me and brings me to my feet.

23

REMEMBRANCE BRINGS REDEMPTION

But ***keep me in mind*** *when things go well for you. Be sure to extend kindness to me by* ***remembering me*** *to Pharaoh. Bring me out of this prison.*
—Genesis 40:14 (ISV)

Memory sure is a funny thing, isn't it? Sometimes Chaim's memory surprises him with some of the things he can remember; other times, it's let him down. For example, Chaim is known among his friends for remembering dates and times with eerie preciseness. Often, they will say, "Tell me what you were doing in March of 2012?" or "Where were you in August of 2014?" or "What was going on in November of 2017?" And Chaim will give details, times, and names—it's all there in his head, ready to be recalled. Yet when he needs to remember something simple and truly important, he cannot. Just the other day, a state trooper pulled Chaim over for speeding. After asking for Chaim's license and registration, he proceeded to ask, "What is your address?" and "What is your date of birth?" Do you think Chaim could remember these things? Not a chance!

The point is, remembering the right things and remembering them at the right time is important for our well-being. But the Scripture teaches us something more. The act of remembering the right thing at the right time is imperative to our journey to fulfill the purposes of God. This is especially true in the most trying of circumstances, when we need God's intervention to redeem what might seem to be lost.

Let's begin by looking at Joseph, who finds himself in prison in Genesis 40. Joseph did not despair over his situation. He spent fifteen years keeping the name of Jehovah on his lips as he moved from a pit to slavery to prison to the position of prime minister of the most powerful nation in the world. After all, he had a promise from the God whose name was on his lips.

Joseph was an inmate in the royal prison, reserved for those who are threat to the kingdom. Egypt had no other prisons. If you violated the law, you were either tortured, enslaved, or put to death; some people experienced all three punishments. However, the royal prison was nothing more than holding cells for political prisoners waiting for their hearing before the pharaoh. They faced one of two possible outcomes: the pharaoh would declare them innocent and set them free, or he would declare them guilty and have them executed. The cupbearer and the baker were there for the same reason as Joseph, waiting for a hearing before the pharaoh to determine their fate.

On that rather disturbing note, let's look at Genesis 40:14 and these words: *"keep me in mind"* and *"remembering me."* Both are the same words in Hebrew, *zacar,* which means "to remember" or "remember me."

In the first use of the word *zacar,* we find it in a construct to the word *im.* This word is used to express *if* or *suppose.* Joseph is expressing this as, "If you can, please remember me." Then Joseph uses the same word, *zacar,* for the cupbearer to make mention of him to Pharaoh. In this case, *zacar* is in a Hiphal form and would suggest that Joseph was not necessarily asking the cupbearer to mention him, but to do something or say something that would cause the pharaoh to remember him. In this context, Chaim would translate this as, "Let's get this thing moving."

Joseph's appearance before Pharaoh is as a foreign slave charged with the attempted rape of an Egyptian—and the wife of a highly respected court official to boot. This left Joseph with little hope of an acquittal and no hope of a plea bargain. Yet he *zacar*—he remembered a dream, a promise from God. And he would rather try to live out that promise or die in the attempt by asking a cupbearer to remember him. *Zacar* not only means to remember but, according to Rabbi Samson Hirsch, a nineteenth-century linguist and Hebrew master, it is used specifically for the remembrance to redeem.

If this is the case, what might a look into the LXX suggest? The Greek word used to translate *zacar* is *mimnēskomai,* which means "to mention," "to take to make known," or "to recall something that might be forgotten." What is relevant and interesting to our study here is that this is the same word used in Luke 23:42, where the thief on the cross beside Jesus pleads, *"Jesus, remember me when you come into your kingdom."* Some scholars suggest that Luke had Genesis 40:14 when he was writing this. It's certainly likely. It's also likely that Luke's audience would recall Joseph's request in the prison as they heard the thief on the cross make this request to Christ. Both Joseph and the thief were pleading for favor when their lives were at stake. Joseph's conviction had all but sealed his fate, and the thief on the cross was certainly doomed. But they understood that destiny was somehow connected to the act of remembering. A simple yet meaningful recollection could ensure that their present circumstance was not their final end. Their remembrance would lead to their redemption.

The cupbearer does in fact remember Joseph, who eventually becomes the ruler of Egypt, second only to Pharaoh. As for the thief, he received assurance that Jesus would remember him and take him to paradise *that very day*. Jesus says, *"Truly, I say to you, today you will be with me in paradise"* (Luke 23:43.) Amēn, the Greek word for *truly,* means "certainly" or "so it will be!" The important thing is where it shows up in this sentence. It comes before the word *today* to emphasize that the thief would inherit more than he hoped for, *certainly on that very day*, all because Jesus remembered him.

The simple act of remembrance is a big part of these two stories. It's part of our story as well. Like Joseph in prison and the thief on the cross, we too may find our circumstances hopeless and wonder if this might be the end of God's purposes for us. The small act of remembering the goodness and graciousness of God in times of sorrow or pain is the first step to experiencing God's redemption and the continuation of God's visible faithfulness in your life. Don't despair. Remember.

Pray this from your heart:

I will remember Your graciousness and faithfulness, my Redeemer, and recall Your promises, which I have stored up in my soul to be recollected in times as trying as these.

24

FOCUS YOUR PRAISE, RELEASE YOUR BURDEN

O God, my heart is ***fixed****; I will sing and give* ***praise****,*
even with my glory.
—Psalm 108:1 (KJV)

Ever have one of those times when you carry a burden that is so overwhelming, you can't even pray? You try to pray, but it is just such an effort, and you feel so weighted down. This is the way David felt when he started to write this psalm. The rest of the psalm appears to be one of his lighter moments. He seems so joyful, so happy. Yet this first verse gives David's true emotions away.

He calls out to God saying that his *heart is fixed*. The Hebrew word for *fixed* is *kon*, which has the idea of being *established* or *directed*. Today we would say his heart was *focused*. Yet not on the good in this case. What David is saying here is that his heart was not focused on God but on his burden. It is for this reason that he will sing and give praise.

In the LXX, we discover that the Greek word used for *fixed* is *hetoimos*. It can mean "to prepare" or "to arrange." In some instances, it could mean "to erect" or "to set up." In 2 Corinthians 9:5, *hetoimos* is used when Paul is talking to his church about an offering they had pledged to the church in Jerusalem. He was sending Titus and two others to

Corinth to pick it up. In light of this, Paul expected the church to make preparations to start arranging this gift they promised so that it might be *hetoimos* or "ready" when Titus and the gang arrived. Hence, the idea of *hetoimos* is attached to the idea of "preparing something," "getting something together," or "setting something up."

If we use what we learn from the Greek, we could say that David is saying, yes, his heart was focused on his burdens, but his focus on his burdens was setting up and erecting all kinds of woes and griefs. He was erecting all sorts of inner turmoil for himself. All of us know a little something about this, don't we? When left to ourselves, our imaginations will go into overdrive and arrange some pretty intense illusions for us that only make our burdens heavier. When we focus on our dilemmas, we prepare further dilemmas.

Perhaps David realized this and so decided to do the exact opposite of erecting grief upon his grief. He chose to sing and give praise.

The Hebrew word for *praise* that is used here is *zamar*. This is a word for "singing a wordless melody," "singing birds," or "a knife used for cutting or pruning." This is a *very focused praise*. The idea of a knife cutting and pruning suggests a precision in cutting away that which is bad and leaving that which is beneficial. Throughout the ages, it has been noted that birds sing to claim and defend their territory, to keep the undesirables away.

Thus, this *zamar* is a praise either in word or song that is meant to ward off, cut off, or prune away anything that is undesirable in David's relationship with God that is hindering his spiritual growth. This is a very direct, very specific praise, with no fluff or disjointed or meaningless words. The word is also in a Piel form with a paragogic Hei, which makes this direct praise very intense.

In the LXX, the word for "give praise" is *psallō*. In essence, it means "to sing a song" and "to celebrate." It is used in several places in the New Testament. In Ephesians 5:18–19, talking to the Ephesian church about the standard Christian life, Paul says, *"And do not get drunk with wine, for that is debauchery, but be filled with the Spirit, addressing one another in psalms and hymns and spiritual songs, singing and* ***making melody*** *to the Lord with your heart."* The words *"making melody"* come from *psallō*. Paul is telling his church that singing songs and celebrating in our hearts unto the Lord must be a normal part of Christian life. It is part of remaining full of the Spirit, which keeps us from serving our sinful desires. When we sing to the Lord, we are erecting praise to Him instead of arranging and preparing an imagination of grief and misery, which breeds anxiety and fear. David puts his whole being into this praise. And Paul urges the Ephesian church to do the same.

As we close this study, a good question to ask is what might this *zamar* and this *psallō* look like?

This worship of David doing a *zamar* was not backed up with blaring music. Rather, it was most likely found alone in the quiet of his chambers, where he could focus on God without any distractions and thus hear the voice of God. This is a praise that David is giving to God through a deliberate effort. Perhaps it didn't come naturally at first. Maybe it was forced and began mostly as rote. But as David becomes more focused on God, his praise begins to become a *zamar* praise, a pruning and cutting praise that cuts through all that burden and stress, removing all his cares. Some call it a sacrifice of praise. You are sacrificing all your cares and burdens for the sake of praising. That is a sacrifice we would gladly make.

The *psallō* that Paul had in mind is quite like David's *zamar*. Though it could be accompanied by instruments, it was to be from the heart. (See Ephesians 5:19.) This refers to involvement from the entire person, which would surely require a deliberate effort. Maybe it may feel a little mechanical at first. Yet eventually, it would lead to a place where every component of the entire person would give way to the Spirit and relinquish its burdens.

Perhaps this should give us a moment of pause. How does this relate to some of the worship we experience in our contemporary, evangelical churches? While we are certainly not out to criticize this sort of worship, we are suggesting that we should be mindful that, no matter how we worship, it should be from the heart and with the entire person, with total focus. That can be a point to think about because our Western culture loves blaring music. What's so bad about that? Neurologists have discovered a portion of our brain that releases a chemical that creates pleasure from music that is played so loud, it almost reaches the point of being painful. That pleasure chemical is released to ease the impeding pain. Perhaps we might say, "Oh, feel the presence of God." Is it though? Or is it just a gland releasing pleasure hormones? Are we giving our whole person to God in *zamar* and *psallō*? Or are we just getting a hormone high?

Whether the music is loud or soft, the point is our worship needs to be focused so we can cut away at our unsanctified imaginations that erect further burden for us.

Is your heart arranging needless dilemmas for yourself? Focus your praise. Offer your whole self in singing and making melody to the Lord. It's certain to bring your imagination under control and will lift your burdens.

Pray this from your heart:

I will focus my praise upon You, Lord. My whole self shall be full of melody as I walk in the Spirit and live this Christian life.

25

MANIPULATING A CAMEL

Thou shalt hide them in the secret of thy presence
*from the **pride** of man.*
—Psalm 31:20 (KJV)

A few years ago, Chaim rode a camel for the first time in Qatar and was surprised by how gentle, calm, and compliant the animal was. He's not sure if the camel realized how much bigger or faster it was, but it sure did listen to him. Well, actually, the camel listened to its owner. Chaim's "camel ride" consisted of the owner holding onto a rope attached to the camel and leading it around in the desert for about a half hour. Yes, it's a tourist thing. It's not like riding a wild camel. The beast's owner had total control over it; the camel had no wildness or will of its own.

This brings us to our verse for this study, where we discover that God is promising to protect us or our goodness from the *pride* of man. This does not sound like too much of a threat at first glance. Why would we want to hide our goodness from the pride of man?

The Hebrew word for *pride* that is used here is *rokes,* which is a rather unusual word to use. Usually when we think of *pride,* we think of the Hebrew word *gavah,* which implies arrogance or a sense of superiority. *Rokes* is not this, but then again, it is very difficult to find an English word to fit this Hebrew word. It has been used for *conspiracy, plots, evil leagues*, and *snares* but the meaning is ultimately dubious. It's a loaned word from the Akkadian for "hobbling a camel"— that is, tying a camel's forefeet and looping the rope around its neck to restrain its movements to train it for carrying burdens or a rider. The owner exercises control over the animal. It's one thing for humans to do this to animals; to exert this power over other humans is something else entirely.

In the LXX, we discover that the word for *pride* comes from the word whose root is *tarassō*. *Tarassō* has a wide range of meanings, including "to shake up" and "to perplex." There are instances in antiquity of this word being used to describe an upset stomach, panic, and mental uncertainty. Perhaps a wider use of the word is to describe an uprising, riot, or public disturbance such as in Acts 17:13. Here, Paul was preaching the gospel in Berea to Jews in the synagogue. Jews from Thessalonica got wind of this and didn't like it too much so they showed up in Berea and began *"stirring up"* (*tarassō*) the crowds:

> *But when the Jews from Thessalonica learned that the word of God was proclaimed by Paul at Berea also, they came there too, agitating and stirring up the crowds.*

The Thessalonian Jews created a civil disturbance through clever manipulation. They took advantage of the good nature of the crowd in Berea in an attempt to get what they wanted. The Thessalonian Jews were treating the Berean citizens like a bunch of camels—needling them and upsetting them for their own benefit and gain.

This gives us a bit more dimension as we look at Psalm 31:20. Perhaps David might be suggesting that God hides us from the manipulation and control of those malicious individuals who would seek to perplex our lives with their malevolent schemes. He won't stand for others taking advantage of our innocence and goodness. David assures us that God desires to keep us from people who want to treat us like beasts.

Perhaps there is a situation in your life where some kind of manipulation is going on, such as mistreatment or abuse in a marriage, a controlling leader at your local church, or something taking place at the professional level. In these times, the Lord promises to hide His people in *the secret place*. The Hebrew word for *secret* is *satar*, which means "unknown things." In the LXX, the Greek word used is *apokryphos*. It means "hidden," but it can have a sense of hidden for the sake of protection or for the sake of preserving something for oneself. It is often used to describe hidden treasures or storing away that which is most precious to you. What the psalmist is saying is that in a manipulative situation, God desires to protect those who are His. He preserves them amidst abuse because they are precious to Him. God acknowledges the value of the person who is being manipulated, though the manipulator does not. God recognizes their dignity, and He draws near during these moments with His presence.

If you've ever experienced God's presence, you know you can find wisdom, joy, and hope there, a way forward in spite of the circumstances. If you are being treated like a beast, press in to the presence of the Lord. There He will cover you and grant you what you need.

Pray this from your heart:

Lord, You hide me away at times from those who would seek to manipulate and control me. My dignity comes from You. Keep me safe in Your presence.

26

A STRENGTH THAT WON'T BE EXHAUSTED

*As for us, our eyes as yet **failed** for our vain help: in our watching we have watched for a nation that could not save us.*
—Lamentations 4:17 (KJV)

What is the longest you have ever stayed awake? Chaim's record is nearly two days without a single minute of sleep. He was on what was literally a trip around the world to teach in Qatar, Ho Chi Minh City, and Kuala Lumpur. During the first half of the trip, he woke up on a Friday morning in Qatar and spoke at a church there. He then flew to Kuala Lumpur at night and landed there the next day. There was no time to sleep. A driver picked him up, and Chaim freshened up at his hotel, and then went directly to another service to speak. Afterward, he went to dinner to celebrate the pastor's birthday. He told his host he didn't think he could stay awake. Yet she insisted. "It's really important that you be there."

Chaim gave it his best shot but he had never been so exhausted in his life. He paced the floor and tried to sip coffee, but nothing worked. Eventually he gave up. He went to the corner of the room, found a table, put his head down—and that was it. Chaim doesn't even remember getting back to his room that night. The funniest part of this story is that the next day, he noticed he had a video on his phone, a 36-second clip of him recording his coffee. Chaim didn't remember this at all, so he asked the pastor's son about it. "Yeah, man," the son said. "It was really weird. You pulled your phone out and were just recording your coffee. It was like you were sleepwalking." Chaim doesn't remember doing that. His strength had failed. His desire to stay awake had given in to exhaustion.

Perhaps this might illustrate something about the hearts of the people in Lamentations 4:17. The Assyrians were ready to march on Judah, but instead of turning to God for help, the Judeans looked to the nation of Egypt to deliver them. Yet Egypt had their own problems; they would not come to deliver Judah. The people placed their hope of salvation in *"an arm of flesh"* (2 Chronicles 32:8).

The words *"our eyes as yet failed for our vain help: in our watching"* in our Scripture reading for this chapter paint a very sad picture. A clearer rendering would be "our eyes have become exhausted watching for the help that never arrived." The word *failed* in Hebrew is *kalah,* which means "to destroy" and "to bring to an end." It also means "to strive" and "to desire." The picture we have in Lamentations 4:17 is one of watchmen standing in their watch tower, anxiously looking to the West for their help to arrive from Egypt while the Assyrian army was preparing for an attack from the East.

The eyes of the watchmen *failed* or *kalah.* They were filled with desire and hope but were becoming exhausted and eventually devastated when their anticipated salvation failed to appear. The hope of the watchmen had given way to exhaustion, like Chaim at the birthday party in Malaysia. It had collapsed in the corner.

In the LXX, the Greek word used to translate *kalah* is *ekleipō.* It often means *failure* in the sense of giving up or running out. It is used in Luke to describe the how the sun stopped shining during Christ's crucifixion:

> *It was now about the sixth hour, and there was darkness over the whole land until the ninth hour, while the sun's light failed.*
>
> (Luke 23:44–45)

Some scholars believe there was an eclipse then. If this is the case, we could say that sunlight failed. It gradually began to fade away and diminish. If you wanted to personify the sunlight, you could say it became exhausted.

When we place our hope and our trust in an arm of the flesh, we are sure to be disappointed. We can try our best to stretch our own strength out as far as it will go, but soon it will fail us. Perhaps there is some instance in your life where you are attempting to trust in your own ability. It might work for a bit, but eventually, you will find yourself in the same situation as Chaim was during that party—doing everything you know how to do, even ridiculous things, to keep from failing.

Have you found that your strength is failing you in ministry or in a relationship that you hold dear? The more you try to hold onto it yourself, the more you may find it slipping away. If that is the case, King David suggests a way forward. In Psalm 20:7, David said, *"Some trust in chariots and some in horses, but we trust in the name of the LORD our God."* When David said this, he most likely remembered that day he stood before Goliath. David did not *kalah/ekleipō* or become discouraged, disappointed, or exhausted while waiting for help from an arm of the flesh. He rested in the power of the name of the Lord.

Maybe you are at that point where your strength can no longer go on. You're at the end of the line. The best thing you can do is let go. Surrender your strength to the Lord and begin to lean on His strength. His strength won't ever get exhausted or require you to do ridiculous things to carry on.

Pray this from your heart:

I turn my finite strength to You, oh Lord, for it is at its end. It has become exhausted. In Your infinite power I now rest, for it is You who fulfills my hope and enables me to carry on.

27

AN INTERVENTION THAT SAVES

Before I was afflicted I went astray, but now I keep your word.
—Psalm 119:67

We run into lot of teaching that God wants everyone to be healthy, and He never brings *affliction* on anyone. People get pretty emotional if you even suggest that God might bring *affliction* on us. Yet parents bring *affliction* on their children all the time, saying things like, "Go to bed and no TV tonight" and "You are grounded." The word *punishment* is often associated with affliction and tends to carry a bad connotation. We would rather use the words *correction, intervention,* or *consequences.* For those who do not like the idea of God bringing *affliction* on us, you could say that God must, at times, bring about an *intervention,* a *correction,* or *allow us to suffer the consequences* of our actions.

Actually, the word for *affliction* in Hebrew is *'anah,* which means being "humbled by life events." This would be correction by God, intervention, or even the consequences of sin. In this psalm, it appears that David is grateful for his *'anah* because it brought him back to the Lord. We learn that he did suffer the consequences for his sins, and he accepted these consequences for he saw it as God *intervening* in his life to bring him back to a right relationship.

This makes us recall the story about Mel Trotter, who founded the Grand Rapids City Rescue Mission and became a well-known evangelist in the first half of the twentieth century. Sometimes he even concluded many of Billy Sunday's crusades, preaching in the tabernacles that he erected. Prior to this however, Trotter was an alcoholic. According to one story, he sold his baby's shoes to purchase a drink. One day when Trotter returned home after a binge, he found his two-year-old son had died. At the funeral, he swore he would never take another drink, but by that evening, he was drunk again.

Trotter wandered the streets of Chicago, homeless, broke, and hopelessly drunk. Then he entered the Pacific Garden Mission, where the Lord not only saved him but cleaned up his life. Trotter went on to direct missions and become a famous evangelist. Many years later, some businessmen took him to an expensive restaurant and told him to order whatever he wanted without worrying about the cost. Trotter ordered soup broth and water. When asked why, he explained that his years as an alcoholic had so torn up his digestive system that he could no longer eat solid food. Trotter's wife tried very hard to forgive his past and work toward a fresh start, but the years of abuse and alcoholism were too much to overcome and led to the end of their marriage.

Christian libraries are filled with the testimonies of people whose lives were changed through the blood of Jesus, yet they still had to suffer the consequences of their former lives. They still had wrecked marriages, children who were in prison or on drugs because they were not good parents, or difficulty in finding a job because of their past record. God never promises to deliver us from the consequences of our sins, only to forgive us.

An exploration into the LXX shows us that the word used to translate *'anah* into the Greek comes from *tapeinoō*. It means "to humble," "to cause to be low," and "to put to shame" or "to break someone's spirit." In antiquity, it could mean to be decimated by military power. This is the typical word used in the New Testament to describe humility. Upon examination of the various places where it is used, what can be noticed is that there are two agents of humbling. Either we do the humbling, or God does. In fact, seven verses tell us this. (See Matthew 18:4; 23:12; Luke 14:11; 18:14; 2 Corinthians 11:7; James 4:10; 1 Peter 5:6.) It's not rocket science: either we make a conscious decision to bridle our lives or God will allow the consequences of our unbridled lives to bridle us. Either way, there is going to be an intervention. The wise man or woman has a self-intervention before facing a forced intervention caused from the consequences of poor choices.

Chris recalls a heartbreaking story that illustrates this. A number of years ago while visiting Spain, he was awakened by a text message from an old friend whom he hadn't heard from since high school. It said, "Check the local news back home." To Chris's surprise, another old friend had been arrested. The police report was shocking. This didn't seem like the person Chris had known years ago. Eventually, the dust settled, and Chris had an opportunity to speak to the man before his sentencing. He wanted to know the pathology behind his behavior. The old friend told Chris, "I was glad when I got caught. It was the best thing that ever happened to me. I didn't want to stop what I was doing. Getting caught finally put the brakes on choices that could have gotten much darker." After serving his sentence, he is now leading a quiet life, free from his detrimental habits.

Ideally, it would have been best for him to bridle his actions. Because he didn't intervene, the law intervened. The sentence he served afflicted his life: he lost his job, his reputation, and his credentials. One could say he was brought low and decimated by the consequences of his choices. But this affliction was also an intervention, a means whereby God offered him mercy. Was it the best possibly solution? No, for he could have bridled himself before it got to that point. But God cared about him so much He allowed the law to intervene. Today, he's alive. That's something to be thankful for.

Consider your life. Do you need to have an intervention with yourself while there is still time? Perhaps you are past that point, and there's already been a forced intervention that's come through the consequences of your action. Will you resent God for this affliction? Or will you embrace it as God working through His mercy with your best, long-term interests in mind?

Pray this from your heart:

I bring myself low, oh Lord, that I might not be afflicted. Your ways are perfect; Your mercy has saved my life.

28

GOD LICKS UP MY PROBLEMS

The L*ORD will* ***fight*** *for you, and you shall hold your* ***peace.***
—Exodus 14:14 (NKJV)

If I see ten problems walking down the road toward me, I can be confident that nine will fall into a ditch before they reach me.
—President Calvin Coolidge

Do you ever face a problem that just saps all of your strength? You cannot concentrate on anything else but that problem. You are unable to enjoy the pleasures of the day, and at night, you cannot even find peace in a deep, restful sleep. Before long, you discover the problem was not even a problem at all. You wasted a perfectly good day fretting over a problem that didn't exist.

How often do you worry over problems that God has chosen to fight for you? Looking at the literal understanding of Exodus 14:14, it clearly tells us to let God do the fighting. We just need to hold our peace.

The Hebrew word for *peace* used here is *charesh*. The word *charesh* is in a Hiphal form. There are two possible ways to express this in the

Hiphal. You could say, "The Lord will fight for you and just keep your big mouth shut." Or you could say, "The Lord will fight for you and you will just go about your business." We would say it can be rendered both ways: "The Lord will fight for you so just shut your mouth, quit bellyaching, and just go about your business."

In the LXX, the Greek word used to translate *charesh* comes from *sigaō*. It means "to be silent" and "to keep quiet about." The emphasis is on the deliberate intention of the individual to actively and consciously choose silence. An example is found in Luke 9:35–36. Peter, James, and John have witnessed the transfiguration and heard the voice of God from a cloud confirm that Jesus is the Messiah. Afterward, "*they kept silent and told no one in those days anything of what they had seen.*" They decided to keep the glorious vision to themselves. Imagine what an act of the will it took for them to keep their traps closed about the whole thing! With this nuance, you could add to the rendering of Exodus 14:14: "The Lord will fight for you so *decide* to keep your big mouth shut and deliberately stop your bellyaching and go about your business."

Maybe as we concentrate on this word *fight,* we may find it easier to *chares/sigaō*. *Fight* in Hebrew is *yilachim*. Amazingly, the root word for *fight* is *lechem,* which is the word for bread or nourishment. When it is used as a verb, it means to feed or devour. The word *fighting* or even the phrase *waging war* may not be an appropriate rendering for *yilachim* in the context of Exodus 14:14. For one thing, in English, the word *fight* suggests the outcome is uncertain. Does God have to duke it out with an enemy? How many punches does He need to get in before the enemy topples? Remember, there can be up to thirty-five English words that would apply to one Hebrew word. So one word in Hebrew has to go a long way.

Also, keep in mind that all words in Hebrew originate as a verb, and the noun evolves out of the verb. Originally, as a verb, *lechem* meant "to eat" or "to consume." The noun form would then be *bread*. Here the verb is in a Niphal form and thus it would mean "to devour." In modern

English, it's the equivalent of licking your plate clean or scraping the bottom of the Twinkie wrapper. God does not square off with our problems and start punching it out while we sit back cheering Him on. He just walks up to our problem and eats it up. "Gulp!"

Yet we just keep saying: "Well, God is fighting for me. God is handling the problem; it will just take time. Poor God, He must really be getting tired, must be the ninth round already." Ah, no! God does not need to duke it out with our problems. The bell sounds, He walks out, and after one punch to the jaw, the problem is down for the count. But that is not *lechem*. *Lechem* is the bell ringing, God walks out, faces the problem, and in one gulp, the problem is history. If God does duke it out with a problem, He is just tenderizing it so it is not so chewy when He devours it. Also, He may not be removing the problem right away if it's going to get bigger. He waits until just the right time to consume it.

The LXX would agree with this. The Greek word used to translate *lechem* comes from the word *polemeō*. It can mean "to make war" and "to attack." In the book of Revelation, it is used twice to describe Jesus making war on His enemies. (See verses 2:16; 19:11.) The overwhelming nuance behind this word is "to ravage." Think of a one-sided contest where the winning side inflicts severe damage and devours the opponent.

When applied to the overall idea of Exodus 14:14, we could think of this Scripture as saying, "The Lord will ravage your enemies and lick them up when He makes war on them. It will be a one-sided contest, so make a decision to keep your big mouth shut, deliberately stop your bellyaching, and go about your business."

You get the point, right?

The best way we can illustrate this is to consider Chris's friend's pet piranha. When Chris visited his friend, he always felt sorry for the little goldfish placed in the tank to satisfy the piranha's hunger. The piranha had razor-sharp teeth and was ten times bigger than the goldfish. The poor little fish never put up much of a fight when the piranha decided it was time to eat. It would get licked up and ravaged.

Your problems are a goldfish. When God moves, He gulps them up, and they're history.

Pray this from your heart:

You fight for me, oh Lord, and lick up my enemies. I have no reason to gripe or complain.

29

SHOW ME YOUR WAYS

Show me Your ways.
—Psalm 25:4 (NKJV)

This seems to be a common heartfelt cry for many Christians. We really just want to be sure we are in the center of God's will; like the psalmist, we are crying out to God to show us His way. There are a couple of popular songs that quote this Scripture. So what exactly does this mean when we sing this? That depends on what the psalmist means when he says: *"Show me."* Our first thought is that the psalmist is actually going to physically see something that will guide him—sort of like an angel appearing and saying, "Okay, just follow me, and I will take you on the way you are to go." Odds are, this will not happen.

This Hebrew word for *show* is *hodi'eni,* which comes from the root word *yada',* an "intimate knowing." The word *yada'* is often used to describe intercourse between a man and woman. The idea is that this kind of intimate union is meant to be the highest and ultimate form of knowing someone. To truly enter into this, a couple must know each other so well that they have no secrets, no hidden agendas. They know things about each other that no one else in the world knows, and they trust each other completely with that knowledge. They enter that relationship only wanting to please their mate, whether they themselves are pleased in return or not. This sort of flies against the norms of our promiscuous society, where everything comes quick and easy. Yet this is what the word *yada'* implies.

In the LXX, the Greek word used is *gnōrizō*. It implies intelligent comprehension of a matter as one becomes acquainted with it. In John 15:15, Jesus says, *"No longer do I call you servants, for the servant does not know what his master is doing; but I have called you friends, for all that I have heard from my Father I have made known to you."* Jesus has told His disciples about God's divine purposes in the coming of Christ. As a result, His disciples became acquainted with God's ways. Look at how intimately the disciples developed in such knowledge. Compare them from the Gospels to the end of the book of Acts. Let's just say the Peter who denied Jesus certainly had grown in the knowledge of God by the time he wrote his epistles! Thus, the writer of Psalm 25:4 is not just asking for a knowledge of God's ways, but to be made intimate with these ways.

Like many people, Chaim thought about trying his hand at direct sales when he was young and reckless. He applied for a direct sales job with a fairly large company with an elaborate screening process. He was *the chosen one* out of a hundred candidates, but he guesses that the other ninety-nine decided this was not their cup of tea. In the second interview, the manager gave Chaim a demonstration package and a script. He was told to memorize that script word for word and not deviate even in one word. The manager said the script was written by a proven sales team and was guaranteed to work. He said those who deviated from the script usually failed in the business, but those who stayed with the script in their presentation were successful.

Chaim discovered that the manager was right, and after that, Chaim joined the non-chosen. There is a way that seemed right to him but in the end, it was a failure. The right way was their way because it was the proven way.

This is why the psalmist is literally begging God to make him very intimate with His ways. He does not want to deviate one moment in the wrong direction because he knows God's perfect way is the right way that will lead to an intimate relationship with Him.

The Hebrew word *hodi'eni* rendered as *show* means to know intimately. It comes from the root *yada'* in a Hiphil imperative form. The psalmist is begging God to cause him to bring about some circumstance that will bring him into an intimate understanding of God's ways. He is looking for a practical understanding of His ways and how they apply to every aspect of his life.

How did the manager convince Chaim that following the script word for word would work and Chaim's way would not? He introduced Chaim to his top ten salespeople, all making six-figure incomes. Each one said pretty much the same thing: "I thought it was foolish to follow a script word for word and when I started I just did it my own way, and it did not work. Once I followed the script, I was amazed that it actually worked."

The psalmist needed no convincing that God's way works; he just needed to know God's way. That is why this word for *knowing, yada'*, is in a Hiphil (causative) imperative (command) form. The psalmist is really asking for a physical, visible demonstration of God's ways. He wants something tangible, like a prophet or a priest whom he really respected as a man of God, someone he could observe and watch his lifestyle and practices.

Had Chaim decided to join that company, he would have had to go through six weeks of training, followed by six weeks of riding around with top salespeople. He could have made a six-figure salary like the others, but he didn't want to pay the price in time, effort, and his own integrity to do it.

To know the ways of God, you must want it so badly that you are willing to become intimate with His ways and make them your life, 24/7, to sacrifice whatever you must sacrifice.

What would *you* sacrifice?

There was a Christian man in a Muslim nation whose wife and daughter were taken from him. He pleaded with their Muslim captors to return his wife and daughter. They said they would gladly do so if he would deny Jesus and become a Muslim; otherwise, they would kill him on the spot and force his wife to marry a Muslim man. He said, "I cannot deny my Jesus. Kill me now." For whatever reason, they did not kill him, but they did force his wife to marry a Muslim man. After six years and much prayer, through a miracle of God, the man was reunited with his wife and daughter.

The word *way* in Hebrew is *derek*. In its Semitic root, it means "a doorway" or "path to someone's presence." In this context, it is a doorway or path to the intimate presence of God. In the LXX, the Greek word used to translate *derek* is *hodos*. This word is quite common in the New Testament and is often rendered *road, path,* or even *journey*. In the Synoptic Gospels, this word is used in the scenes when Jesus and the disciples are going from one place to the next. (See Matthew 21:8; Mark 11:8; Luke 9:57.) Yet the word is also used to describe a manner of life, even Christianity itself. (See Acts 19:23.) It can, then, mean a divinely ordained course. Combined with the Hebrew, we see a divinely ordained path to the presence of God that is a way and manner of life for those who choose to walk it.

It is like in a marriage relationship. The spouses choose a new path and a new way of life. They leave their path of blessed singleness to share a new journey whereby they care for another person and eventually have children. The Jews actually say when you are married, you are "born again." So it is with our relationship with God. If we really want to be intimate in our relationship with Him, we must be willing to make the sacrifice, change our way of life, and enter a journey that leads into God.

So the next time you sing, "Show me Your ways," remember that you are offering God a heartfelt prayer to grow intelligibly into the knowledge of the divine manner of life He has prepared for those who choose to follow Him.

Pray this from your heart:

I choose Your way of life, Lord, that I might know You intimately. May I journey with You.

30

THE TUNING FORK

Good and upright is the Lord;
therefore he instructs sinners in the way.
—Psalm 25:8

Some years ago, we had a "God is good" explosion. All over Christian television, you kept hearing "God is good." It seemed that in every church and every church service, we were singing that chorus "God is so good, He's so good to me."[4] When we hear that someone is good, we think of someone who is kind, moral, and decent, yet sort of average. Even in our English language, we have *good*, *better*, and *best*, with *good* being the lowest on the totem pole. Elementary school grades often consist of: U = Unsatisfactory, F = Fair, G = Good, E = Excellent, and S = Superior. Good is average, somewhere between Superior and Unsatisfactory.

But come on, when we talk about God, we are not talking average, passable, or decent; we are talking about the greatest, the ultimate, the most wonderful. We hardly apply the word *good* to God, but the Bible says He's good—not excellent or superior, but at least not fair or unsatisfactory.

4. Paul Makai, trans. Marilyn Foulkes, "God Is So Good," 1970.

All throughout the Old Testament, everything was just good. The world was created as good, animals were good, man was good. In English, however, that meant average, that there was something better out there.

So here we are once again in Psalm 25:8, confronted with the knowledge that God is just good and upright, you know? Average, right up there with us. If we look at that word *good* in the Hebrew lexicon, what we find is the word *tov,* which means *good, pleasant,* and *agreeable.* Again, that is pretty much average, nothing really special. Yet in the Bible, the word *good* is always used in reference to something valuable, special, unique, or wonderful. One rabbi explains that if you examine all the renderings of the word *tov,* you find that at the very core is the idea of something musical, something that is in tune or in harmony.

This moves the word *tov* out of the realm of opinion. We can argue about whether a burger is good, for example, but whether something is out of tune or in harmony is not a matter of taste or opinion because it can be measured.

If we examine the Greek word chosen to translate *tov* in the LXX, we will discover that it hints at the idea of something being in tune or in harmony. In Greek, there are a number of words that can be used to describe "good." Here *chrēstos* is used; it means "usable," "pleasant," and "in order." In antiquity, it is used to describe an orderly house instead of one in disarray. If you are a neat freak and have mild obsessive-compulsive disorder like Chris, you can appreciate this. Chris is so tidy, he has a designated space for everything. If one thing gets moved during the day, he puts it back in place before he goes to bed at night. He likes to know that everything is in harmony with his idea of order.

When we take what we have learned about the word *chrēstos* and apply it to *tov* rather than *good,* we find something that makes much more sense. When God created the world, He placed it into harmony with Him. When we say God is good, we say that He is the harmonizer, the tuning fork by which everything is measured.

So we learn in Psalm 25:8 that God is that great Harmonizer, and He is upright. The word *upright* in Hebrew is *yashar,* which means to be *straight, level,* or *correct.* In the Greek, the word used to translate *yashar* is *euthēs,* which is part of a word family that carries the idea of *straightaway, smooth,* and *right.* If God is *yashar/euthēs,* then all He does and says is correct, level, and right. When a piano is perfectly tuned, it is correct. God is not only the ultimate Tuning Fork by which all creation is measured, but if you are in tune with God, then all you do and say is correct.

Being good and upright will not get you into heaven, but being in tune with God so you do the correct thing will. This can only be accomplished through the blood of Jesus Christ. Then in heaven, you will be another harmonious instrument for the kingdom.

Think about this: an orchestra has many different instruments playing at the same time. When the musicians tune up before a concert, it sounds horrible until they all harmonize and then begin to play as one. If just one instrument is out of tune, it will throw the whole orchestra off and create an unpleasant sound. Heaven will be like a mighty orchestra with everyone in tune with the Master, the Maestro, who died and shed His blood so that He could bring everyone into harmony with Him. Only Jesus Christ can make you *tov*—good, or in tune with Him. Only then can you belong in that great orchestra hall that we call heaven.

Pray this from your heart:

Tune me, Lord, that I might be in harmony with Your right ways and live in accordance with the order of Your creation.

31

INTERCEDING IN THE BATTLE

Whenever Moses held up his ***hand****, Israel* ***prevailed****, and whenever he* ***lowered*** *his hand, Amalek prevailed.*
—Exodus 17:11

As a kid, Chaim and his classmates used to play a game in gym class called Medic. It was everyone's favorite. It was essentially dodgeball, but there was a *medic* on each team who would revive everyone who had been hit by a ball and thus were out of the game. The medic would pull the player across the gym floor to the base to get them back into the game. As soon as the opposing team discovered who the medic was, everyone began aiming for them. Then the game would change. Everyone started to protect the medic because if the medic was out, it was just a matter of time until the game was over. The medic was interceding for the rest of the team.

As funny as it might sound, this kind of illustrates Exodus 17:11.

Some have suggested that Moses holding his hand up was sort of like a battle flag. In the heat of battle, you are not sure whether you are winning or not; you are just concentrating on the business of staying alive. In the American Civil War, each regiment had two flags, representing the country and the regiment. The flag carriers were called color guards. The position required bravery because the color guards were unarmed and had to stand in the midst of battle. When things got very confusing in battle, soldiers would rally around the flags. If the flag was still flying, the army was still fighting. We're not sure if that was the practical reason for Moses keeping his hand holding *"the staff of God"* in the air. (See Exodus 17:9.) Whatever the reason, the use of certain Hebrew words here would indicate something a little deeper, particularly the word *yad* for *"hand."* Exodus 17:11 suggests that it was Moses's hand being held up that was important rather than his staff.

Let's take a look at this word for *hand*. If this were a battle sign, the Hebrew should have used the word for *arms*. To use the word *yad* or *hand* would suggest something quite spiritual was taking place. The word *yad* is spelled Yod, Daleth. This combination of letters suggests that the hand is a doorway through which the power of God would flow. When Moses worshipped God, as all Jews did, he did it with uplifted hands.

Chaim read something interesting in the Talmud in Rosh Hashanah 29a. Here we learn that it was not only the physical act of Moses holding up his hand that initiated God's help. It was also the means by which Moses communicated to the Israelites to keep their thoughts turned upward to God and subject their hearts to the will of God. This was the direct cause for God's help.

The word *yad* can also mean to *certify, ensure, verify, confirm* or *authenticate*. The hand certifies the power of God. Hence, we perform the act of laying on of hands when praying for healing to *certify* or *authenticate* the power of God.

It's important to note that when Moses's hand was uplifted, the army of Israel *"prevailed."* The Hebrew word for *prevailed* is *gavar,* which means "to become strong." When Moses lifted up his hand, the army of Israel became strong. Like the medic in Chaim's gym game, Moses was interceding for his team. Life was flowing through him.

The Hebrew word for *prevailed* is spelled Gimel, Beth, Resh and shows that this is a spiritual strength; this is strength to help others (Gimel) that comes from the power of God (Resh) that fills our heart (Beth). These men were not fighting for themselves; they were fighting for their families and their people. With that intent, God filled them with His power or strength.

The Greek word for *gavar* in the LXX is from the Greek *katischyō*. It is a pretty common word in the LXX and means "to gain the mastery over." Its root, *ischys*, makes it part of a word family that suggests "capacity," "superiority," and even "military might." It's uncommon to find *katischyō* in the New Testament, but one particular place of interest is in Matthew 16:18, where Jesus tells Peter, *"And I tell you, you are Peter, and on this rock I will build my church, and the gates of hell shall not prevail against it."* A number of interpreters have looked at this verse in various ways. Chris thinks the simplest and most accurate way of understanding this is that Jesus is telling Peter He is building a new community of believers and death is never going to be able to swallow them up. Death will not be able to "gain the mastery over" those who will rise in Christ. Death will never be superior to the church of God. Here we see a people, the church, who are filled with the spiritual strength that comes from the living God to overcome death.

Perhaps it's not going too far to suggest that if the readers of Matthew were familiar with this word, they might connect its use in Exodus 17:11. When the power of God was working in the Israelites' army, Amalek's army could not prevail against them. Because of the power of God that flows to the church, the enemy cannot gain the mastery over it or ever become superior to it. Moreover, when one of God's own is interceding like Moses, the enemy cannot prevail over that intercession.

Another important point, however, is that when Moses lowered his hand, the Israelites started to lose strength. Again, like the medic, if Moses became weak, their team would start to lose. The Hebrew word for *lower* is *navach,* which is in a Hiphil imperfect form. In this case, it would mean "to cause to rest." When something caused Moses's hand to rest, the army started to lose.

Moses' very actions controlled the outcome. This is very significant for us. We may not be on the front lines of the spiritual battle, but that does not give us cause to sit back and take it easy. Just as Moses stayed in worship with God during the battle, interceding on behalf of his army, so too are we required to intercede on behalf of those who are fighting spiritual warfare.

We have seen Christians who are very eager to throw rocks at their pastor or other Christian leaders when they succumb to a lust of the flesh. But the enemy knows that if he can attack and defeat your leader, you will be easy pickings. If you have not had your hands lifted up to God, interceding on that leader's behalf for the spiritual battle, then you are just as much to blame and should be held accountable for that leader's defeat. We are all responsible to protect the medic. We can do this by praying for and supporting those who are interceding in the battle.

Pray this from your heart:

I pray for those, oh Lord, who are in the midst of the battle right now. Grant them strength to overcome so that the enemy cannot prevail.

32

THE PATH OF TRUTH

***Lead** me in your **truth** and teach me.*
—Psalm 25:5

The psalmist is asking God to not only lead him in His truth, but to teach him truth as well. The age-old question is, "What is truth?" Obviously, the questioner is not asking for the dictionary definition of truth but the *nature* of truth. There are many definitions of the English word *truth*. Basically, it is conformity with fact or reality. To a philosopher, it is the actuality of existence.

Nothing gets Chaim's boiler fire burning hotter than when someone opens their Bible, points to a verse and says, "But this is truth." This is particularly irritating when he interprets the verse entirely differently than the other person does. The Word of God is truth, but is your interpretation or mine the truth? Both interpretations seem to conform to reality, but both cannot be truth. Now, if that person points to the name *Jesus* and says, "That is the truth," there can be no argument there.

Jesus said in John 14:6 that He is *"the truth,"* meaning He is the actuality of existence. Why do we exist? What is our purpose in life? It is knowing Jesus, for He draws us into the God who created us. When you create something, you have a reason for that creation. Truth as defined in this context is the reason, the actuality of and for our existence.

Does that English definition fit the Hebrew word for truth? The word *truth* in Hebrew as used here is *ba'amiteka* from the root word *'emth,* which is spelled Aleph, Mem, and Taw. Aleph is the first letter of the Hebrew alphabet and Taw is the last. Truth is the beginning and the end. In the middle of the word for truth, or the beginning and the end, is the letter Mem, which represents the revealed knowledge of God. Truth is the knowledge of God from the beginning to the end. Truth is everything about God.

The word itself is defined in our lexicons as *faithfulness, firmness, reliability, stability, endurance, sureness* and *divine instruction.* That is a lot of good things. No doubt the psalmist desires to be led in all these things. Don't we all? In its Semitic root, the word means "a firmness that is completely trustworthy." In our vernacular, we would say, "It is a sure thing."

In the LXX, the translators chose to translate *ba'amiteka* with the Greek word *alētheia.* This is the most common word for truth in the New Testament. It means "reality that's sure." You know, things that we are certain can be trusted, such as the sky is blue, the grass is green, turtles move slowly, and vanilla ice cream is delicious on apple pie.

God sent His Son Jesus, who is the living example of the sure thing. He is the one who can guarantee life, for He is life eternal. Jesus said, "*I am the way, and the truth* (*alētheia*), *and the life. No one comes to the Father except through me*" (John 14:6). Jesus is saying His way is the surest guaranteed manner of life, the one that leads to life eternal. By following Him, He will lead us to the Father.

The psalmist wants to be led into the *surest thing.* The Hebrew word for *led* is *derek,* which means a "manner of one's lifestyle." We have already examined this word in our studies and have seen that it also means a *doorway* or *path* to someone's presence. In the LXX and in the New Testament, we have seen that the word comes from *hodos,* which means *road, path,* or *journey.*

The psalmist is firmly demanding that God cause something to happen to bring him into a lifestyle that is the surest thing to God's presence. He wanted a doorway and path to God's reality.

Do you ever want to live a life that is the surest thing to the life God wants you to live? That could mean that God will take your sunshine and turn it into a storm. Do you want that life badly enough to enter a storm? It may mean that God will take joy and turn it into sorrow or turn your wellness into pain if that is what it is going to take to smash your will and bring you into the manner of living that is pleasing to God. Are you willing to do that? Do you want it that badly?

Fanny Crosby became blind as an infant due to a physician's mistake. After many years of walking with God and writing some of the world's most beautiful and soul-stirring hymns, she was asked by a reporter what she would say to the physician who caused her blindness if she ever met him. She said, "I would thank him." She believed with all her heart that her blindness brought her into that *derek/hodos,* that doorway, journey, or manner of walk or lifestyle with God that brought about the thousands of hymns and gospel songs that were a blessing to millions.

We can read Psalm 25:5 as, *"Lead me in your truth,"* but we must remember the emotional context and the broader meaning of the words *lead* or *derek/hodos* and *truth* or *'emth/alētheia.* For then, we will capture the true heart of the psalmist who is crying out to God: "Do something in my life that will give me a path to a lifestyle that is pleasing to You and is a sure thing to Your presence." Just remember that embodied in this demand is the risk of a sacrifice of your will, desires, and lust.

During one of the most trying periods of his life, Chris went to a pastor friend of his and started to rant. He cried out about all the injustice, all the pain, and all the hurt, rejection, and suffering, and then concluded by saying, "It seems I've lost everything and all I got was Jesus in return." Chris's friend simply said, "Amen." So it will be. Truth!

Pray this from your heart:

Do something in my life, oh Lord, that gives me a path to a manner of life that pleases You, that is a sure reality to Your presence.

33

A BURNING HEART

If I say, "I will not mention him, or speak any more in his name," there is in my heart as it were a ***burning fire*** *shut up in my bones, and I am weary with holding it in, and I cannot.*
—Jeremiah 20:9

Jeremiah faithfully preached an unpopular message that people did not want to hear. As a result, he was persecuted and thrown into prison, where he made his complaint known to the Lord. He had grown tired of always having to preach an unpopular message only to be rewarded with persecution. He was tired of being the good soldier. Jeremiah even said he had decided not to mention God anymore. He was just going to forget about God and go his merry way, like bringing a bad romance to an end.

Except Jeremiah cannot stop talking about God because He *"is in my heart as it were a burning fire."* Burning fire in Hebrew is *kaesh bo'eret,* which in this context is a destructive or all-consuming fire. In Semitic literature, a *kaesh bo'eret* or "consuming fire" is a metaphor for passion. Jeremiah allowed God's heart to enter his heart, which means he also entered into God's heart and felt a *consuming fire.* He felt God's passionate love. When God's heart joined with Jeremiah's heart, he felt the power of God's consuming passion such that he could not abandon God's call on his life.

When we examine the LXX, we discover that the Greek word for burning comes from *kaiō,* which means "to consume" and "to ignite." It is used quite frequently in the New Testament, but one place of particular interest is in Luke 24:32, when the two disciples walking on the road to Emmaus encountered Jesus. Prior to this encounter, they were a bit confused and anguished about the events that had taken place concerning the Lord's crucifixion. (See Luke 24:13–24.) Perhaps they were somewhat frustrated like Jeremiah. After having recognized that the Person they were talking to was Jesus, they admitted that when He spoke, their hearts burned within them. (See verse 32.) This suggests that their time with Jesus was emotional and had infused them with a passionate, zealous love that they didn't have earlier when they were feeling disappointed. The presence of Jesus had left them changed and filled them with inner conviction that they so needed. The fire of God had been reignited in these two individuals' lives. God's heart entered their hearts.

In the next verse, they take decisive action. "*They rose* ***that same hour*** *and returned to Jerusalem. And they found the eleven and those who were with them gathered together*" (Luke 24:33). The Greek words *tē autē hora* ("that same hour") can be translated "at once" or "immediately." This indicates God's passionate love had not only filled them but had stirred them to action.

Have you ever felt a burning, consuming fire, a *kaesh bo'eret,* or has your heart ever *kaiō* in God's passionate love? Such a burning cannot be experienced from reading a textbook, studying in the seminary, or even going to conferences and attending workshops. It comes only through a genuine encounter with the living God.

Chris has felt a burning or consuming fire for God a number of times in his life. His most profound experience of this reignited passion occurred while he was on a trip to London. He was scheduled to speak at a conference for five nights. On the way there, he was a bit concerned because he didn't have a single sermon written out. He had no idea what he would speak on. Chris almost felt like an imposter and wondered,

"Am I in any position to be preaching these services, cold and unprepared as I am?"

That night around 2 a.m., the presence of the living God filled Chris's hotel room. He woke up startled. As he relates, "And when I say that my room was filled with glory, I am making an understatement. It was exactly how I have heard it described—*weighty* and *heavy*. I wept. I sobbed. I was afraid to move. I just sat there in silence, and something in my heart began to catch fire. Like Jeremiah, God's heart was entering my heart."

That evening, with almost no notes, Chris stood up to preach his first sermon for that event in London. Yet the power of God filled the entire auditorium. There were tears of repentance that led to salvation, which led to Spirit baptisms. There even were healings. What had moved Chris? What had caused the change? What had prepared him? God's heart had entered his.

Perhaps you aren't a minister and think you would never have this sort of opportunity to experience God's heart. But you do. Chris often shares how he made a deal with God that if He would weep for Chris when his heart was broken, Chris would weep for God when His heart is broken. Since that time, there have been a number of occasions when God drew Chris into His heart, and he could feel God's passionate love, His *kaesh bo'eret* and His *kaiō*.

Chris recently encountered a sour, nasty individual who kept criticizing him. Chris told the Lord that if this person uttered one more disparaging remark, Chris was going to overhaul their engine. But God drew Chris into His heart, and Chris felt God's passionate love, His consuming fire and broken heart for this person. Chris was so overwhelmed by this consuming fire, he couldn't hold it in. He struggled mightily to hold back tears although he had promised God that he would weep when His heart was broken. Chris tried to cover the tears but this individual noticed them and misunderstood. They thought they pushed Chris too far and apologized. But God's love and broken heart led to the tears, not the nasty remarks. It was God's *kaesh bo'eret* and His *kaiō*—His consuming fire or passionate love.

Like Jeremiah, when we want to just forget about the name of God and when He seems unresponsive to our pleas for help, God opens His heart to us, and we begin to feel His consuming fire or passionate love. Like the two on the road to Emmaus, when this happens, we enter His heart. We are changed and reignited, which causes decisive action that makes us live our lives with conviction. And that is convicting to the world around us.

Pray this from your heart:

Ignite me, oh Lord. Let Your heart enter my heart that I might live my life with compassion and conviction.

34

ACCEPTING GOD'S INVITATION

The Spirit of the Lord GOD is upon Me, because the LORD has anointed Me to preach good tidings to the poor; He has sent Me to heal the brokenhearted, to proclaim liberty to the captives, and the opening of the prison to those who are bound; to proclaim the ***acceptable*** *year of the LORD, and the day of vengeance of our God; to* ***comfort*** *all who mourn.*

—Isaiah 61:1–2 (NKJV)

Have you ever been to a party only to realize you weren't invited? There's no more awkward feeling. Chaim was recently at a get-together where a friend brought someone who was unknown to anyone there without asking the host for permission. This presence of the uninvited guest made the entire event awkward from start to finish. It was clear that the unexpected guest felt every bit of that awkwardness. Their face looked like they wanted to crawl into a hole and not come out. It made Chaim realize how important an invitation is. It's an approval and authorization to be somewhere, which is both a joy and a relief.

In Isaiah 61:1–2, the prophet discusses a time when God would invite people into His kingdom. Isaiah calls this *"the acceptable year"* of God. He is not speaking of a particular year but a period of time. The

Hebrew word for *acceptable* is *ratzah,* which means "to be welcomed or invited to an event or into one's home." In the LXX, the Greek word used to translate *ratzah* comes from *dektos.* It means *approval* and carries the idea of being approved to be in someone's company. It's like the feeling you have when you show up at a party and you know that you belong there. In the New Testament, this word is used in Luke 4:24 when Jesus is talking about the ministry of the prophet after reading Isaiah 61:1–2 for those in the synagogue in Nazareth. He says, *"Truly, I say to you, no prophet is acceptable (dektos) in his hometown."*

Jesus is aware that prophets in the Old Testament—God's messengers—were rejected and dishonored by their own people. They were treated like uninvited party guests. With this in mind, we can understand that God's acceptable year is a particular time when God welcomes His people and accepts them into His family through the redemption of their sins. It means the *approval* to be in His family and to be part of His kingdom. It's favor with Him. God wants you there, and you are aware that you belong.

Many Bible scholars believe that Jesus is echoing Isaiah 61 when He gives the Sermon on the Mount. This sermon speaks of the coming of God's kingdom and stands as an invitation into it. Moreover, He essentially quotes from Isaiah 61:2 when He says, *"Blessed are those who mourn, for they shall be comforted"* (Matthew 5:4). In saying this, Jesus is describing the appropriate response for His invitation into His kingdom. The invited guests are to *"mourn"* or *bewail* their sins so much so that they turn from them, enabling them to enter God's kingdom and be comforted.

In Isaiah 61:2, the Hebrew word for *comfort* is *nacham,* which means "to console." In the LXX, the Greek word used to translate *ratzah* comes from *parakaleō.* It means "to encourage" and "to call to one's side." This was used in military contexts to encourage soldiers. Soldiers have been through the worst of life and have seen the darkest things that war has to offer. In the same way that an officer might encourage a soldier to carry on despite their war experiences, the Lord encourages those who mourn in repentance to move forward despite having been through and participated in the dreadful life of sin.

Yet there is something else in Isaiah 61:1–2 and Matthew 5:4 that should not be overlooked. In both passages, this mourning seems to not only be for our sins but also the effect they have on God. When we dishonor someone or break their heart, we are breaking the heart of someone whom God loves. If a child comes home to their mother and crawls up into that mother's lap, weeping with a broken heart because of some bully, is that mother's heart not broken as well? Has that bully not awakened momma bear, who will come charging after the bully because her child's heart is broken, which has broken her heart as much if not more?

When we realize that we have broken the heart of someone God loves, we should also realize that we have broken the heart of God as well. And then we understand that we do not deserve God's invitation into His kingdom—yet He still invites us anyway. What mercy! He draws near to our repentance and encourages us to continue forward into His will despite the ugliness of our sin. This is the power that takes place when His invitation is met with our repentance.

Perhaps this explains why some of the most hardened men end up becoming the most faithful members you can find in a church. Chris recalls one man who used to attend the same church he did when he lived in Minneapolis. Prior to this man's conversion, he was a detached father who drank away his life at a bar. The church's outreach team ministered to him one night on the streets. Through that team, God invited him into His kingdom. For the first time, he sensed God's acceptance—the acceptable year of the Lord. This was met with his own mourning and regret over the ugliness of his sin. His drinking had hurt both his daughter's heart and God's heart. But God filled him with His Spirit and worked through the Spirit to bring restoration to those areas of his life that sin had made ugly. Afterward, as a member of the church, he was always there—Mr. Faithful, you could call him. He never missed outreach night and served faithfully in his auxiliaries. He was aware that he belonged in the family of God and was a part of His kingdom. Mourning had met invitation.

Pray this from your heart:

May Your invitation be met with my mourning, oh Lord. Your mercy has granted this time of acceptance. I belong in Your kingdom.

35

HE LEADS US BESIDE STILL WATERS

He makes me lie down in green pastures.
He leads me beside ***still*** *waters.*
—Psalm 23:2

Many of us have experienced a peaceful time along the shores of a lake, river, creek, or ocean. Chaim's father was an avid fisherman who loved to leave the city and find a little lake, river, or even a creek to just sit and fish. Chaim soon began to suspect that catching fish was more of an excuse to get away from the hustle of city life and spend time in the tranquility of the waters of rest—*menuchot* in Hebrew. Chaim and his father would travel to Canada, taking the highway all the way to its end. From there, they would take an old dirt loggers' road. Sometimes they would have to stop to clear the road or repair an old decrepit bridge that looked like it could barely hold a person, let alone an automobile.

At the time, it was an adventure; today, Chaim thinks back and wonders, "Was my dad nuts or what?" Yet when they made it all the way to the end of that so-called road, to what seemed like the end of the world, there was a crystal-clear lake surrounded by wildlife and woods. Not another soul in sight. Then Chaim's father would take their rowboat and go out clear to the other end of the lake. There they were, totally off the grid, and a physical change came over his father as he stared out over that lake. He gave off a sense of true peace and serenity. Chaim often imagines that God was just encompassing or surrounding his father.

This illustrates the imagery found in Psalm 23:2. Here, David says that God leads him beside still waters. *Still* in Hebrew is *menuchot,* which literally means rest as in "waters of rest," like the serene crystal lake that drew Chaim's father.

The word *manuchot* comes from the root word *nauch,* which means "to rest," "to cease from activity," and "to relax." We discover this nuance of the word when we explore how *"still"* is translated in the LXX. The Greek word that is used comes from the word *anapausis*. It means "to stop," "to cease," "to relax," and even "to get away from trouble," which would mean finding relief. If this word sounds familiar, it's because its root, *pauō,* is part of the word family from which we get the English word *pause*. This word can imply a stilling of the soul in such a manner that causes refreshment of the inner man. In the New Testament, Jesus uses this word when He speaks about what it is like to follow His teachings regarding His kingdom. He says, *"Take my yoke upon you, and learn from me, for I am gentle and lowly in heart, and you will find* ***rest*** *for your souls"* (Matthew 11:29). Jesus is telling His audience that following Him will refresh their inner man and bring relief to their souls because Jesus would care for them even to the point of laying down His life for them. What a contrast this is to following the legalistic ways of the uncaring religious leaders who burdened the people with their rigid demands. (See Matthew 23:4–7.)

In looking at Psalm 23:3 and Matthew 11:29, it's not going too far to suggest that when we follow the teachings of Jesus—when we become His disciples—He leads us away from trouble into a place where our souls throw off every burden and find rest and refreshment. When you obey the teachings of Jesus, it's like taking an old road away from hustle and bustle to a crystal lake where there is peace and serenity. If you think about it, it's not all that complicated—obeying the words of Jesus brings rest. Disobeying produces anxiety and panic.

Chris recalls a time when he was counseling someone who was oppressed by some kind of dreaded emotional state. It was so severe that this counselee had to take various medications in order to sleep. When they were awake, they were as nervous as can be. In a counseling session, Chris asked the person to consider their obedience in relation to the teachings of Jesus. Were they showing mercy to others? Had they been holding grudges and living with anger? Were they seeking vengeance? As they went through the list, the person began to realize that they had disregarded a lot of what Jesus had taught about the kingdom, and their inner soul suffered. They didn't need hot yoga, cold plunges, or essential oils to return to homeostasis. They simply needed to do what Jesus said. Of course, this story isn't meant to oversimplify every issue and problem humans have, only to suggest that a lot of our own inner turmoil and anxieties can be quenched by obeying Jesus. He leads us to still waters, and our obedience is choosing to follow Him there. As soon as this counselee repented and began to obey the Lord, their inner state completely changed...and they no longer needed medication to sleep.

There is one more thing worth noting in Psalm 23:2. *Nauch,* the Hebrew word for rest, is closely related to the Hebrew word *manach,* which means "to give, as in a sacrifice." A secondary meaning is that God leads David besides *sacrificial giving waters.* The word for *water* is *miy,* which can be a noun or the interrogative word *who.* Chaim believes David carefully chose his words under the inspiration of God to give us two messages in one. Not only did David say that God leads us beside waters of rest to bring us peace, but there is a little play on words here so that he is also saying, "He leads me to the one who will make a sacrificial gift which will bring me to eternal rest."

Of course, the teachings of Jesus bring us inner peace. But we should also note that it is the sacrifice of Jesus that has given us eternal peace with God. His death on the cross has solved the problem of sin and reconciled us to our Creator.

Inner peace, peace with God, still waters—this is the result of following the only One who can bring rest to our souls.

Prayer this from your heart:

I will obey Your teachings, which bring refreshment to my soul, my Lord and God.

36

CAST YOUR BREAD UPON THE WATERS?

Cast your bread upon the waters,
for you will find it after many days.
—Ecclesiastes 11:1

In Ecclesiastes, we have a verse that might be familiar to some of us. Perhaps we have heard it when a preacher takes up an offering. They may say that when you cast your bread (money) into the offering plate, after some time, it will return to you tenfold. Those are good returns. This giving and getting more in return sounds like a pretty good deal. But is that really the idea?

We're not sure the idea of *casting* fits with throwing money into an offering plate. In fact, the word "cast" in Hebrew is *shalach,* which is more about placing something rather than throwing it. In the LXX, the Greek word *apostellō* is used to translate *shalach.* This word comes from the same Greek word family in which we get the word *apostle.* It means "to send away," "to let something free," and "to send something away with a special purpose." It isn't just a nominal sending, like sending a random email. Rather, the sender has an attachment to the thing he sends and is somehow connected to it, like sending a precious gift. *Apostellō* is used all over the Gospels and Acts. For instance, in John 17:18, Jesus is praying to the Father and says, *"As you* ***sent*** *me into the world, so I have* ***sent*** *them into the world."* Jesus was precious to the Father, and the Father sent Jesus into the world with the special purpose of bearing witness to God's love. Moreover, the disciples were precious to Jesus, and Jesus sent them into the world with the special purpose of bearing witness to Christ's love. The point is, *apostellō* was a special sending in which the sender was profoundly connected to the item being sent.

As such, the idea of placing your precious bread on the water and sending it away seems like a strange exercise. Why would you do that? Wouldn't it become useless and soggy? How could it even reappear?

This is supposed to be divine advice?

This passage was written by King Solomon, one of the wisest men in the world. The Jewish Midrash Rabbah tells the story behind this verse that helps us understand its true meaning and the valuable lesson it has for us.

When King Solomon was building the Temple, there was a certain type of material that he desperately wanted to use. However, this material could be found in only one place in the entire known world, a small kingdom not too far from Israel. Solomon sent emissaries after emissaries to this small kingdom, asking the king to name his price for this material. But the king refused to sell the material to Solomon. After many delegations went and returned empty-handed, King Solomon himself gathered his servants and royal guard together and went personally to plead with this king to sell him the material he so desperately wanted.

Even the appearance of the richest and most powerful king in the world could not persuade the king of this small realm to give up the material. After a week of negotiations, King Solomon gave up and decided to return home. As his men were packing to leave, a servant told Solomon that the other king wished to see him. When they met again, the king told Solomon he could have the material—in fact, he could take all he wanted. How much was he charging? "Nothing," the other king said. "Take all you want as a personal gift from me."

What brought about this change of heart? The other king explained that a few months earlier, when he had gone to war, his only son was taken captive and imprisoned. Just a few days prior, his son managed to escape and started to cross the desert. Starving and weak, the son almost died… until he came upon an oasis. As he was drinking some water by the stream there, he noticed a bundle carefully wrapped and *shalach/apostellō* (placed) in the water, bobbing up and down in the ripples. Unwrapping the bundle, he found it filled with enough food to revive his strength and bring him home.

King Solomon immediately discerned that this king was offering the material as a gift to his own gods for saving his son. Solomon explained that he worshipped a different God, the God Jehovah, and he could not accept the material for the Temple of his God.

The king replied, "You misunderstand. This is not a gift to my gods." Then he pulled out a blanket and said, "This is the blanket my son found the supplies in that he needed to survive." Pointing to a Star of David embroidered on the blanket, the king said to Solomon, "That is your symbol, is it not? It was you who left that bundle of food that saved my son's life."

You see, there is an ancient Middle Eastern custom still practiced today in the desert. Whenever you come upon an oasis, you will always find a bundle of food. If you need it, take it. If you don't and you happen to have a surplus, take some of your precious bread and *shalach/apostellō* (let it free) to serve a special purpose—to feed those who might come along and be in need. You never know when *you* will be the one in need.

We have a similar system today in many retail stores, where you find "Leave a Penny, Take a Penny" dishes. The idea is to leave your surplus pennies or other change for someone in need, or take a few coins when *you* could use some.

And that is what Ecclesiastes 11:1 is all about. It is not giving because you expect to get a windfall in return. It is freely offering what is precious to you to help others out because one day, you may need that very same help from others.

Pray this from your heart:

May I have a heart that offers freely what is precious to me, oh Lord. As You are generous, may I be generous as I will need generosity in return.

37

TOUCHING THE UNCLEAN

Command the children of Israel that they ***put out*** *of the camp*
every leper, everyone who has a discharge,
and whoever becomes ***defiled*** *by a corpse.*
—Numbers 5:2 (NKJV)

At the end of World War II, the British were approaching a Nazi concentration camp. Fearful of what the British would find and wanting to buy some time to clean up their crimes, the Germans sent a delegation of officers with a white flag to inform the British general that there was an outbreak of typhoid fever. They suggested that the British just bypass the camp. Both sides agreed not to shoot at each other, and the British almost fell for the Germans' ploy. But as they were walking past the camp, the stench caused the British to have second thoughts. That's when they investigated and discovered the horror that the Nazis tried to cover up.

The ancients had no concept of microbes, but they probably knew that encountering a diseased person might pass that defilement onto them. They considered sickness to be a punishment for disobeying God. In fact, a whole school of ancient Jewish teaching developed around the reason for laws like the one in Numbers 5:2.

At one point, the Pharisees condemned Jesus for not demanding that His disciples wash their hands before eating. They were astonished that Jesus did not wash His hands either. The Pharisees knew nothing about hygiene, only that the disciples were breaking *"the tradition of the elders"* (Matthew 15:2), which later became the Talmud. This *tradition* was basically a commentary of the Torah or man's opinion, not Scripture. This tradition taught that during the night, demons entered your body and then gravitated to your hands—for after all, it is with the hands that evil deeds are done. But demons hate water, so the tradition taught that you could inadvertently ingest demons unless you washed your hands before you ate.

In the Gospel of Luke, Jesus heals a leaper, heals a woman with an issue of blood, and raises a person from the dead. (See Luke 5:12–16; 8:43–48; 8:40–56.) The Jews were familiar with Numbers 5:2; these three types of people were considered outcasts, yet they are the very ones whom Jesus touched and healed. We think Jesus was making a statement here.

Maybe it seems cruel to separate these poor people from others. The word in Hebrew for *put out* is *shalak,* which means "to send away," for a purpose. It is used for a messenger being sent forth with his message. In the LXX, the Greek word comes from *exapostellō*. It can mean "to be sent away on a mission or to fulfill a purpose." It wasn't just a heartless banishment but a means to achieving a better end. We learn later in Scripture that there were priests who were assigned to care for those who were unclean. They would lay hands on them and pray for their healing. If they were healed, they would have to go through a cleansing process. No one could touch a leper, those with a discharge of blood, or those who came into contact with a dead body except the priest. They were not cruelly cast aside but put into quarantine, thousands of years before the purpose of this isolation was known and understood. It was believed that something had entered them that made them unclean.

These sick people were said to be *defiled* or *tame'* in Hebrew. Some translations render this as simply *unclean* or *ceremonially unclean.* The word *tame'* comes from a Sumerian word for *pollute*. It means to take something that is pure and good and add something that takes away or destroys that goodness and purity. In the LXX, the Greek word used to translate *tame'* is *akathartos*. This is another word that begins with an alpha privative, so that the "a" before the word cancels out what comes after it. In this case, the Greek word that comes after the "a" is from *katharos,* which means "spotless," "without blemish," or "free from any defilement." Hence *akathartos* means *defiled, foul,* and even *lewd*. This is the typical word used to describe evil or unclean spirits in the Gospels. (See, for example, Matthew 10:1; 12:43; Mark 1:23–27; 3:11; Luke 4:33.) But interestingly enough, it is never used in the Gospels to describe an individual who is afflicted with a demon.

It is also interesting that Jesus was not considered a priest, yet He touched each individual before they were healed. He did not need to touch them, but He did. This must have shocked those who believed that the demon would come off the individual and onto Jesus or that the illness would pass onto Him. Some thought Jesus must be demon possessed because He touched the sick and people who they thought were sick from demonic activity.

You see, when Jesus reached out and touched these people who were *tame'/akathartos* or *unclean,* He was trying to show that what He created was good and pure, but the enemy brought something that was bad and made it impure. *Pollute* may be the best word for this. When we think of pollution, we think of pure water or pure air that God created being poisoned.

Knowing this, it is especially important that we recognize that all human beings contain the divine image of God in them, despite their sinfulness and the choices that they make that are influenced by the demonic. When we encounter such individuals, we should remember that Jesus was not afraid to initiate an encounter with them by acknowledging their dignity as humans created in God's image. Jesus's touch was a way of recognizing their humanity, value, and worth despite the uncleanly affliction that had come upon them. We can do the same. A touch of dignity might very well be the first thing those who are afflicted need to find the healing and restoration that comes from their Maker.

Pray this from your heart:

Touch me, oh Lord, and I shall be clean. Make me acceptable in Your sight, my God and Maker, whose image I bear.

38

IN HARMONY WITH GOD'S HEART

*Create in me a **clean** heart,*
O God, and renew a right spirit within me.
—Psalm 51:10

Years ago, an orthodox Jewish rabbi showed Chaim a special room in his house. It was filled with books about God, including commentaries on the Torah, the Talmud, the Mishnah, and the Targum. The rabbi picked up one book and said, "You Christians, you read the Torah like any book outside this room. You must read the Torah with your heart and then you will understand the words God spoke through David." That struck Chaim: "The words God spoke *through* David."

So he began to read the Psalms as if they were his own heart cry. As Chaim came to Psalm 51:10 and examined his own heart, motives, and longings, he realized how far he was from God and longed for that *"clean heart."* He began to feel what David must have felt in his heart. David had committed sins that had separated him from the presence of God. It wasn't the consequences of his sin that troubled David; he was willing to accept those. In fact, under Jewish law, David should have received the death penalty since he committed both adultery and murder. The prophet Nathan told David that he would not die and was indeed forgiven. (See 2 Samuel 12:13.) But David's heart was broken over the separation that his sin had caused between him and God. You would think that having your sins forgiven and the consequences removed would be enough—and perhaps for many of us, it is enough. We think, "Well, my sins are forgiven, and I'm on my way to heaven. Praise God! Hallelujah!" But David was still left with a broken heart.

The Talmud tells a story that may explain David's broken heart. A king had a son whom he loved very dearly. He willingly granted his son's every request. However, the son became disobedient and would not submit to his father's corrections. Finally, the king called a servant and commanded him, "Whenever my son needs anything, let him ask you, and you must give to him generously." The servant asked, "But why give him anything if he is disobedient?" The king replied, "I love my son, and I don't want him to be in need. However, I cannot look upon him in his disobedience, so he cannot come to me with his request. I will grant his request through you so I do not have to look upon him."

Maybe for some of us, it is enough that God still answers prayers, still provides for us. But for David, that was almost irrelevant. He wanted much more. David's heart was broken because the God he so loved could not look upon him. So he cried out to God, *"Create in me a clean heart."* Just what was he asking for? The Hebrew word for *clean* is *tahor,* which means to not only cleanse but to purify so it's made pure and ready for absorption.

David wanted his heart to be so purified that it would be absorbed by the heart of God. Rabbi Samson Hirsch, the nineteenth century linguist and Hebrew master, relates the word to harmonization. David wanted his heart to harmonize with God's heart, to be in perfect tune with God's heart so that David could imitate every note God sang and repeat it in his own life. He did not want to do anything that was not in total synchronization with God. Perhaps this is what Jesus echoes in Matthew 5:8 when He says, *"Blessed are the* **pure** *in heart, for they shall see God."*

In the LXX, the Greek word for *pure* is *katharos,* a word we have examined already. It means "innocent" and "freedom from impurity." In antiquity, it was used to indicate metals that were without defect, gold that was untainted, and clear crystals, something pure that is undivided. In Matthew 5:8, a *pure* heart describes a heart that follows Jesus with an exclusive loyalty, being in complete harmony with Jesus and His kingdom by obeying His teaching. Thus when we pray for a *"clean heart,"* not only are we asking the Lord to cleanse us from our former sins, we are asking God to share His heart with ours until we are totally absorbed by it, making our allegiance exclusively His.

If you are a football fan, perhaps you remember Barrel Man, a Denver Broncos fan who was voted by *Bleacher Report* as one of the top super fans in modern sports history. For thirty years, Barrel Man, the late Tim McKernan, made it to almost every single Broncos game wearing nothing but an orange drum, cowboy boots, a hat, and suspenders—no matter what the weather. Perhaps the hardest part was that he couldn't sit the entire game.

The gimmick began in 1977 when a family member bet McKernan $10 that if he wore a barrel to the game, he would get on TV. It just so happens that the Broncos made it to the Super Bowl that season. Did Barrel Man's cheering help? Perhaps. He was a devoted fan until his death in 2009. His legend lives on in the History Colorado Center state museum, where there's a statue of Barrel Man and a replica of his barrel for visitors to try on.

McKernan had a pure heart for his team—undivided, totally absorbed, exclusively loyal. He was in sync, dialed in, and in harmony with the Broncos. Next time you ask for a pure heart, think of Barrel Man.

Pray this from your heart:

Create in me a heart that is in harmony with Yours, oh Lord, that I may follow You exclusively and be loyal to Your ways.

39

HAND IN HAND WITH GOD

I am my ***beloved's****, and his desire is for me.*
—Song of Solomon 7:10

When Chaim was just a young man, his dad taught him that a welcoming, firm, confident handshake makes a good first impression. Chaim even got a little hand grip to strengthen his hand to ensure that his handshake was solid. To this day, when he shakes hands, he wants to get it right. Nothing is more frustrating to Chaim than botching a handshake.

Shaking hands is a pretty widespread custom. But have you ever thought about where it comes from? Historians have a number of theories. One is that it allowed strangers to show each other that they were unarmed. Another theory is that the actual handshake, motioning up and down, was a way to shake loose any daggers or contraband the other person had up their sleeve. The handshake was a sign of peace. Both parties were coming together and forming a friendly bond so there was no need for weaponry.

It's all up for debate, but one thing that can't be denied is that a handshake is a sign of friendship and even loyalty. The earliest depiction of a handshake, going back to the ninth century BC, shows an Assyrian king and a Babylonian ruler engaged in something like a handshake to form an agreement. Such images are found all throughout history, even in ancient Rome, where a handshake was depicted on coins.

The point is, if someone shakes hands with you in sincerity, they usually have your best interest at heart. Informal contracts are sometimes formed with just a handshake, while wounded or broken relationships are often healed with a handshake. It is a sign that you are allowing someone to share your space, and you are willing to consider trusting them.

In Song of Solomon 7:10, we discover an interesting word: *beloved*. We learn that God's desire is toward us. But how so? That word *beloved* in Hebrew is *dodi*, which is where the name David comes from. It's really a form of the word *yadiyad*, which means "beloved friend." The word *yadiyad* is the Hebrew word *yad*, meaning *hand*, repeated two times, meaning "hand in hand." This is our idea of a handshake. Thus the word *beloved* gives us the same impression as that of a handshake: God is friendly and peaceable toward us through a bond of intimacy. In other places in Scripture, God is often pictured as extending His right hand, a gesture of rapport and goodwill.

This coincides with the Greek translation of *dodi* in the LXX. It is the word *adelphidos*, which comes from *adelphos*. *Adelphos* means "brother," "companion," and "fellow member." It is the common Greek word for "brother" in the New Testament, being used well over three hundred times. In Philippians alone, it is used nine times in just four chapters. Interpreters have often called Paul's message to the church at Philippi "the friendship letter" because of this. In fact, Paul ends his letter with particular intimacy, saying, *"Greet every saint in Christ Jesus. The brothers who are with me greet you"* (Philippians 4:21). Paul wants a warm, friendly environment in the Philippian church, one in which there are bonds of loyalty and affection between believers who lay down their weapons and form relationships filled with peace and harmony. Having pastored a church, Chris gets this. Nothing takes more out of a pastor than seeing his people fight—and nothing does a pastor's heart better than to see his people come together in genuine friendship and offer each other loyalty.

God has reached out to us with His hand (*yad*). In response, we give Him our hand (*yad*). The result is *yadiyad*—hand in hand, which forms a bond, a beautiful relationship that makes us God's beloved, His friend.

Chris says one of the most meaningful handshakes he's experienced in his life is the first one he ever received in Italy. He arrived at the airport in Catania, Sicily, to speak for a church. It was his first time teaching in Italy. He didn't know any Italian and had no clue how to find his way around. After getting his luggage, he looked around to try to spot his ride, a bit frustrated because he wasn't quite sure who he was looking for. Suddenly, the crowd parted, and a gigantic rotund man looked at Chris with a smile in his eyes. He stuck his hand out and as they began to shake hands, the man forcibly pulled Chris to his chest. Chris felt like a small planet being drawn into a star's orbit. The man began kissing Chris's neck and speaking ecstatically in Sicilian. Then he pushed Chris away, grabbed him by the face, smiled, and started smacking Chris's cheeks.

This was the beginning of a beautiful friendship.

Little did Chris know, *everyone* in the church would show him that kind of love and friendship that entire week.

God, through Christ, has initiated a friendship with us. He sticks out His hand and waits for us to accept through our faith and repentance. When we do, He draws us to Himself and shows us mercy and grace—tokens of His friendship.

Remember that you are God's beloved. He has offered His hand for you to shake.

Pray this from your heart:

Your hand in my hand, oh Lord. I accept Your offer of peace and Your invitation to companionship.

40

A PLACE UNTO THE LORD

And he came to a certain **place** *and stayed there that night, because the sun had set. Taking one of the stones of the* **place***, he put it under his head and lay down in that* **place** *to sleep.*
—Genesis 28:11

"But," he said, "you cannot see my face, for man shall not see me and live." And the Lord *said, "Behold, there is a* **place** *by me where you shall stand on the rock."*
—Exodus 33:20–21

There are a lot of places in the Bible. Ever pay attention to how much geography there actually is? The most tedious class Chaim took as an undergraduate student was Bible geography. It was basically a class about the maps you might find in your Bible after the book of Revelation. The Bible makes a big deal about places. And why shouldn't it? If you think about it, places are important to us…and to God.

Genesis 28:11 is a very curious verse with the use of the word *place* or *qom* in Hebrew. Jacob met God here in a vision of a ladder running from earth to heaven. The text tells us that Jacob "*lay down in that* **place** *to sleep.*" *Qom* in Hebrew means "an establishment" and "claiming rights." This is the same word used in Exodus 33:21 after Moses asked to see the glory or lovingkindness of God. (See verse 18.)

In each one of these verses *qom* is preceded by a definite article like "the." This was not an arbitrary spot, but a special place, a self-existing place. Jacob was to lay his head down upon a rock in this special place. The Talmud teaches that this is the same place that Abraham offered Isaac up as a sacrificial offering. It is also the place where the holy of holies sat in the temple. Jacob called the place "Bethel" or "the house of God." This word *qom* means more than just a place or an establishment; it is a cherished place, a place where close friends who share a history together go to connect. Hence, it is a special place where we go to meet God. Sure, God is with us all the time, but He also has these special places where we can go to escape from the things of this world and just rest with Him in a loving relationship, to share our hearts with each other. Just like two close friends who have been apart will meet again in a place with familiar nostalgia. It's a meaningful place where the friendship flourishes.

Years ago, when Chaim was going through a very difficult time in his life, he was given permission to go into a warehouse at night, after it closed down, so he could spend time alone there to worship and pray. All he had to do in return was clean the little office space. After many days, Chaim discovered a special spot right by the loading docks. In that *qom,* that place, he instantly felt the presence of God. When Chaim stepped out of that spot, that overwhelming presence of peace and joy diminished. In that *qom,* he could meet with God in a special way to share his heart with Him.

Chris's special place is a beach in the Turks and Caicos Islands (TCI) called Grace Bay. He first discovered this beach in 2010 when he was invited to speak for a church in TCI. The church began to have Chris come to teach almost every year, so soon, he had a history with it. Now, after almost fifteen years, he has noticed that he has made some of the most crucial decisions of his life on this beach. Recently, he had to make one of the biggest choices of his life. He needed clarity. So he paused his life, got away from the rat race, and went to his *Bethel* to meet with the Lord. As soon as he started his stroll along the beach, a familiar nostalgia came upon Chris, along with a familiar presence. He got his answer…and a whole lot more.

In the LXX, the Greek word used to translate *qom* is *topos*. It has a wide range of meanings, including *land, area,* and *region*. Essentially, it is a general location of any sort. In the Gospels, there is an interesting allusion to the Old Testament idea of a meeting with the Lord in a specific place. John records that Jesus often met with His disciples in a specific garden:

> *When Jesus had spoken these words, he went out with his disciples across the brook Kidron, where there was a garden, which he and his disciples entered. Now Judas, who betrayed him, also knew the **place**, for Jesus often met there with his disciples.* (John 18:1–2)

In the Greek, the word *place* has the definite article attached to it like the Hebrew word *qom* in Genesis 28:11 and Exodus 33:20–21. It is a very specific place that happens to be a garden. There is no question that this echoes Genesis, when God would meet Adam, His friend, in the garden in the cool of the day. (See Genesis 3:8.) Then, the Creator was meeting with the progenitors of the first creation in a specific garden. In John, the Creator is meeting with the progenitors of the new creation (the disciples) in a garden. By giving us this detail about Jesus and His disciples, John is giving us a hint about what Jesus is up to: He is in the process of bringing about a new creation through His work on the cross. Satan's plans, through Judas, would not interfere with this.

We can see that even the disciples of Jesus had a specific location where they would meet with the Lord. What took place in those meetings in that garden? What would have been said? Think of all the questions they would ask the Lord and the things the Lord would tell them. What a special place that would have been, almost like Eden. These meetings with Jesus, in this garden, prepared them for the apostolic work in front of them that enabled the missionary efforts of the gospel and, as a result, the blooming of the new creation.

Places are a big deal to God. They are part of His purposes for humankind, for redemption, and for us.

Do you have special place where you meet with the Lord? A specific location where He shares with you as a friend? One you can enter and experience a familiar nostalgia and a well-known presence? A place where the friendship has always flourished?

Of course, we have our local churches. These are places where we gather corporately and meet the presence of God. This is why we are encouraged to meet together in the house of the Lord. (See Hebrews 10:25.) But there are also private places where we encounter the Lord out of the priesthood of our own hearts. You do well to consecrate both. Set them apart. And don't forsake them.

Pray this from your heart:

Meet with me, oh Lord, in this place. For this place is the place where I have encountered Your presence.

41

THE BITTERNESS OF OUR LONELINESS

Turn to me and have mercy, for I am **alone** *and in deep distress.*
—Psalm 25:16 (NLT)

Language has created the word loneliness to express the pain of being alone. And it has created the word solitude to express the glory of being alone.
—Paul Tillich

Paul Tillich was one of the most influential theologians of the twentieth century. He believed the philosopher asked the questions, and the theologian found the answers. He developed a systematic theology in which he attempted to answer the problems of human existence that were raised by contemporary existentialists. Tillich believed the questions raised in the philosophical study of ontology, the study of being, could be addressed through the revelation of Christianity.

Tillich would have made a great linguist because he was always breaking down words into their smallest context. For instance, he used to say, "God does not exist." That would startle most people until he explained that existence meant a beginning and an end, and God has no beginning.

Psalm 25 was written by King David when he was fleeing from the palace because his son Absalom has risen up against him, forcing David into exile. (See 2 Samuel 15:12–17.) David was not *alone*; he had a battery of servants and faithful followers with him. He was surrounded by his true friends, not fair-weather friends who offered their loyalty to whoever could give them their status in life. Yet when David cries out to God, he says he is *alone*.

The word *alone* in Hebrew here is *yachid*, and it is truly contextual in this passage. Translating a word in an emotional context is rarely done within our English language because we in the West are very unemotional people compared to the Semitic people. We are scientific and technological in our thinking and therefore judge according to our minds, whereas the Semitic people made their judgments according to their hearts.

So we must examine Psalm 25:16 with our hearts and try to understand what it feels like to be a king whose own son wants him dead. What kind of suffering was David going through at this time? You put all of that in context, and you have your definition for the word *yachid*. The lexicon tells us that *yachid* means "to be united," "to be one," or "solitary," but those definitions do not fit the context here. *Solitary*, perhaps, but Tillich believed *solitude* expresses "the glory of being alone." Another English word that is used for *yachid* is *forsaken*. Yet David was not quite *forsaken* as he was still surrounded by his best friends and devoted followers.

There is only one other English word used for *yachid* that comes inches closer, but no cigar. It is the word *lonely*. This is almost accurate, but we need to add some nuance.

Let's take an example from the life of one of Chaim's friends. She was devastated when her husband passed away. He had taken care of all the financial affairs. One day, she had security, a home, and an identity.

Then practically overnight, her home went into foreclosure, and she ended up homeless, living out of her car. Finally, after finding a temporary place to live on the eve of the first anniversary of her husband's passing, when her grief was most pronounced, she was in a car accident. She was forced to deal with police, insurance companies, and other people—things her husband used to handle. The night after the accident, as she reflected on her husband's passing, she was feeling *yachid*. This was not just being alone; it was the sorrow and pain that come with being alone. It was at this point that her heart cried out like David's, "*Turn to me and have mercy.*"

In the LXX, the Greek word used to translate *yachid* is *monogenēs*. It the LXX, it has various uses but in Psalm 25:15 (Psalm 24:16 in the LXX), it means *deserted* and *alone*, including the sorrow and bitterness of this sort of experience. In the New Testament, *monogenēs* is used in a number of passages, all of which deal with parents who have only one child who is in severe need, endangered, vulnerable, or deceased. This includes a young man in Nain who was the only son of his mother (Luke 7:12); Jairus's only daughter who was dying (Luke 8:42); a man in the crowd whose only son was seized by a demon (Luke 9:38); and Abraham who offered up his only son in obedience to God (Hebrews 11:17). While the word *monogenēs* strictly describes the uniqueness of each child being the sole offspring of their parent, it's peculiar that there is an element of sorrow and pain involved as well as the prospect of the parent ending up alone without their child. In each case, imagine the sorrow and pain that you would experience when the life of your only child was at stake. Yet like David, these parents looked to God for mercy, and God showed it to them: He raised the widow's son at Nain (Luke 7:14–15), raised Jairus's daughter (Luke 8:54–55), delivered the boy who was seized by a demon (Luke 9:42), and spared Abraham's son (Hebrews 11:17–19; Genesis 22:12–13).

Yet what is interesting is that the term *monogenēs* is also used to describe Jesus as God's only Son. (See John 1:14; 3:16, 18; 1 John 4:9). The only Son of God was constantly threatened and made vulnerable.

If anyone was ever lonely like David, it was the Man of Sorrows and the Suffering Servant. In the end, He suffered and died for the sins of the world.

Going back to Psalm 25:16, we discover that *"Turn to me"* in Hebrew is *panah elay. Panah* has the idea of "presence" or "to make an appearance." David was asking God for assurance that He was with David in his bitter loneliness. In the Gospels, we see God turning to His people to meet them in their times of despair. Even Christ, who endured death, was not abandoned by His Father, who raised Him from the dead.

As for Chaim's friend, despite her despair, she recognized that God had turned to her. Speaking of her accident, she said, "His angels protected me."

In the bitterness of our loneliness, when all seems to be threatened or even lost, we can ask the Lord to turn to us. He is familiar with our sorrow. He will show us mercy, however that might come.

Pray this from your heart:

Turn to me, oh Lord, for I am alone. My despair is too much. Be with me in the bitterness of life, when all seems lost.

42

SATISFIED WITH LENGTH OF DAYS

*With **long life** I will **satisfy** him and show him my salvation.*
—Psalm 91:16

The ninety-first psalm is one we all know and love so much, especially when we get on an airplane. Chris quickly learned this one when he began flying between Minneapolis and Detroit during his Bible college days. As soon as the plane hit that turbulence over Lake Michigan, he started to quote this verse.

And yet he's often had a problem with it too. It appears from reading this verse in every modern translation and commentary that if we trust God, keep our eyes on Him, love Him, and bond with Him, we will have a long life. But in other nations, there are so many Christians who are bonded with God and face persecution and death at a relatively young age. What about Christian children who were beheaded by ISIS for declaring their love for Jesus? Does this verse not apply to them? Do they not deserve a long life for their love for Jesus? Does it only apply to those who are lucky enough to be born in a land where they do not have to face death for their faith?

Even in this land, Christians die early deaths. Chris recalls a young woman from his first pastorate who was married with a small child and had a deep love for Jesus. She developed cancer and died at age twenty-four. Why was she not granted a long life? Chris doesn't think the rendering of this verse stands up to the simple facts of this life on earth. History is filled with many devoted believers who died at an early age. Think of Keith Green, a gifted Christian musician during the Jesus movement in the 1970s whose love for Jesus just poured out through his music and his life. He refused to make any money off his records and would often just give them away or tell someone to pay whatever they wished. But this gifted, talented believer who loved Jesus with all his heart died in a plane crash at age twenty-eight. Did this promise in Psalm 91:16 not apply to him?

If we're honest, we've all had these sorts of questions about Psalm 91. We can either back away from those questions or rethink the meaning of verse 16.

There is another way to render the verse that makes more sense and offers a wonderful promise. The phrase *long life* in Hebrew is *oreke yamim,* which literally means "length of days." "*Long life*" is an inference made by translators. This is followed by the Hebrew word *'asabi'ehu* from the root word *saba',* which is rendered as *satisfy.* One rabbinical source renders this as, "He will fill our days with satisfaction."

In the LXX, the Greek used to translate *oreke yamim* comes from *makrotēs* (length) and *hēmera* (days). The word *satisfy, 'asabi'ehu,* comes from *empiplēmi,* which means to fill something up. It was often used to describe eating and drinking until someone has had their fill. For instance, it describes the crowd who had eaten until they were full when Jesus multiplied the fishes and the loaves: "*And when they had eaten their* ***fill*** (*empiplēmi*)*, he told his disciples, 'Gather up the leftover fragments, that nothing may be lost'*" (John 6:12). It seems that the Greek can be understood in light of the aforementioned rabbinical source: God will fill up the length of our days, and we will be satisfied.

The idea here seems to be qualitative and not quantitative. It's suggesting a superior quality of life for those who fear the Lord and trust in Him, not necessarily living life until you get tired and decide it's time to pop your clogs.

This can be a hard pill to swallow in the West, where we have so many advances in medicine and a multibillion-dollar wellness industry. The result is that Westerners no longer *see* death. In the previous centuries, by adulthood just about everyone would have experienced the death of a sibling or a parent. They would have mourned them, buried them, and hoped in the resurrection in order to see them again. That's just not the case now; people don't think they need a robust theology of death or even the resurrection. Our culture has taught us to hold on for dear life as long as we can, which allows us to push back the question of death—and, ultimately, the hope of the resurrection—for as long as we can. This mentality affects the way we read Scripture, giving us reason to find texts that will support our quest for longevity. But even a hundred years ago, people weren't reading Psalm 91:16 with the idea that they could live to be one hundred and twenty years old!

Yet if this verse is read qualitatively, it can be applicable to readers in every century, no matter what their quality of life might be.

The fact is that every day has meaning. There is a purpose to each day of life that God grants to each human. Lamentations 3:22–23 (KJV) are very profound verses when viewed in the Hebrew:

> *It is of the LORD's* ***mercies*** *that we are not consumed, because his* ***compassions*** *fail not. They are new every morning: great is thy faithfulness.*

In Hebrew, *mercies* is the word *chasad* and *compassions* is the word *racham*. These are two words that describe the depths of God's love. Every ticking moment is a treasure filled with *chasad* and *racham*. And in each moment, we have a chance to discover that treasure and experience a new depth of God's love.

So if someone's life is shorter than another's, it doesn't mean their life got cut short. Did they experience God's mercies and compassions in the life they had? Were they filled and satisfied by the depths of His love? Those are the most important considerations.

Pray this prayer from your heart:

Satisfy me, oh Lord, with the depth of Your love all the days I live on this earth. May I recognize Your mercies and compassions in every moment You have gifted me.

43

FIRE ON THE ALTAR

Fire shall be kept burning on the **altar** *continually;*
it shall not go out.
—Leviticus 6:13

When Christians think of an altar, we think of the stairs leading up to the place where the preacher and his chosen sit on the platform. Some think of it as the pulpit. Some churches have a little table just below the pulpit where they put the communion trays or an open Bible. This is considered an altar although it is really just a communion table.

Our English word *altar* comes from the Latin word *altare,* which reflects the Hebrew for "burnt offerings." The Hebrew word for altar is *mizabach,* from the root word *zabach,* which comes from an old Akkadian word meaning "a place of slaughter." Perhaps the preacher could explain the Hebrew understanding of an altar: "Come forward to pray at this altar, which is a place of slaughter where your old life is put to death in exchange for a new life in Jesus."

In reality, the *mizabach* was nothing more than a big furnace. It was the largest piece of furnishing in the tabernacle, the place where the blood sacrifices were made. Picture a square box made of bronze from which God sent a flame from heaven to light a fire within. From the moment it was first lit until the temple was destroyed by the Babylonians in 607 BC, the priests were commanded to put wood in the fire every morning to keep it going and make sure it never went out. It was quite a chore to find wood in the desert—a full-time job for certain priests.

Chaim read something interesting in the Talmud regarding the *mizabach*. In Eruvin 63a, it says, "Although a fire descended from heaven upon the altar, it is a *mitzvah* (good, praiseworthy deed) to add fuel by human hands to keep the fire producing." Chaim believes the Talmud is teaching that the fire sent from God is a picture of the godly fire that burns within every soul. It is the task of the priest to feed and preserve that fire in the lives of people. And if we believe in the priesthood of every believer as New Testament Christians, then it is our responsibility to keep that fire of God burning in each other by feeding it. If that fire goes out in any believer, it is our fault; we have failed in our role as the priesthood of the believer. In other words, God lights the fire in the altar of our hearts, and we continually fan the flames.

When we come to the LXX, we discover that the Greek word used to translate *altar* is *thysiastērion*. It is the word for "altar" or "place of sacrifice" in the New Testament. In Revelation 8:5, we meet the aforementioned *thysiastērion* (altar) again, only it is in heaven. At this point in Revelation, we are in the first of three sets of judgments, known as the seal judgments. There are seven seal judgments and, by 8:5, the seventh seal judgment has just opened. An angel is seen at the altar. He has a censer, and God gives him the prayers of the saints to offer upon the altar.

The smoke of the saints' prayers rises before God. The angel takes his censer and fills it with fire from the altar and throws it onto the earth. The result is that there are peals of thunder, rumblings, flashes of lightning, and an earthquake. Scholars all agree that this is theophanic language to describe the coming of the Lord. It is language borrowed from Sinai, when the Lord met with Moses. (See Exodus 19:16.) In Revelation 8:5, this language signals the coming of the Lord to vindicate His people and bring justice.

What is undeniable is that there is a connection between the prayers of the saints upon the altar and the fire that was thrown to the earth from the altar. It seems as though the prayers of the saints *caused* the fire from the altar to be thrown to the earth, resulting in the coming of the Lord. The saints had been praying for God to bring justice, to come and rule the earth, and to deliver the earth out of the hands of the wicked. Not a single one of these prayers is wasted. God answers with fire from the altar, which symbolize the effectiveness of the saints' prayers. And He returns with justice.

These aren't sloppy prayers. They are genuine, heartfelt intercessions. And while the saints make these out of the priesthood of their own lives, they are keeping the fire of God burning both in their own lives and in their Christian communities. They fan into flame God's desire for what is right, holy, and true—things like justice, repentance, vindication, mercy, and the kingdoms of the earth belonging to Christ. The text in Revelation assures the saints that this endeavor is not futile. The prayers of all the saints of all generations goes up in smoke before the Lord. And God will sooner or later answer by fire from the altar: He will return.

We will be part of His victorious return. But until then, we should fan the flames of our own souls with righteous, heartfelt prayers. We should be mourning the innocent who lose their lives in senseless acts of violence and asking God to right these wrongs. We should be weeping for those all around the world whose lives are taken because of war and natural disaster. We should cry out when it seems like wickedness prevails, both in our personal prayers and corporately with our local churches. As we burn, the incense continues to climb. The angel collects it. Soon our prayers will be complete, and His kingdom *will* come.

Pray this from your heart:

Let the prayers of my heart be incense to You, oh Lord, climbing up before Your altar. My heart is on fire, and I share Your desires. Come in righteousness.

44

PURSUING THE DESIRE OF THE LORD

*But his **delight** is in the **law** of the* L*ORD*,
and on his law he meditates day and night.
—Psalm 1:2

When Chaim was in third grade, his teacher phoned his parents with the news that he had been trash-talking his classmates on the playground. Yep, recess basketball had gotten that intense. Chaim happened to be one of the better players in the class, and he wasn't afraid to let his classmates know it. It wasn't enough for him to score more points than the others; he had to rub it in. Chaim was in pretty deep trouble. First, he received a spanking, then he was grounded, which for a third grader meant no Sega on the weekend with his cousins. Instead of playing *Sonic the Hedgehog* and *Street Fighter,* Chaim's dad had a special punishment for him. He handed Chaim several pencils he had just sharpened and yellow lined paper with Proverbs 16:18 (KJV) written on it: *"Pride goeth before destruction, and an haughty spirit before a fall."*

"You will be writing this out two hundred times today," he told Chaim.

Two hundred times?!

That's devastating news for an eight-year-old. Not only did Chaim think about how his Saturday had gone down the tubes, he also wondered how badly his wrists were going to hurt.

As he wrote, he didn't really stop to think much about what he was writing at first. But somewhere around sentence fifty, he began to wonder about pride and how it would cause someone to fall. He started to ask, "What does a haughty spirit look like?" and "What is the opposite of pride?" and even "Why are pride and haughtiness a person's doom?"

By the time Chaim was finished, this verse had become engrained in him. Today he realizes it might very well have been one of the most important Saturdays of his childhood. It had established in him a desire to live humbly…if for no other reason than because he knew if he didn't, it was just a matter of time until he would be headed for doom.

God's law had taught Chaim something. And he realized, maybe for the first time, that the law of God had his best interests at heart. He decided he wanted to pursue and strive for what it had taught him all the days of his life. He was determined not to be the cocky third grade basketball player anymore. God's law isn't something condemning or harsh. No, it is a lifesaver!

The vast majority of modern English translations of the Bible render the Hebrew word *Torah* as *law.* Yet many Jewish rabbis choose to render *Torah* as *instructions* or *teachings.* These words are more accurate translations of *Torah* than *law. Law* conjures up the idea of courts and police officers. *Teaching* and *instruction* create the picture of classrooms where one learns about life and the way the world functions. Failure to follow the law results in punishment. Failure to follow instructions and teachings merely results in failure.

The psalmist tells us that a man of God *delights* in the law or *instructions and teachings* of the Lord. And why not? Who is better at teaching us to navigate the temptations of life than the One who created life and understands the temptations that come with it? The Jewish people *delight* in the instructions of God so much that they spend their lives *meditating* on them.

The Hebrew word for *delight* is *chapats,* which we understand from our Christian lexicons and Bible dictionaries means "to find pleasure in." Yet it has a much broader meaning. Jewish linguists see *chapats* as related to the word *chapash,* which means "to seek." *Chapats* is a much stronger form of *chapash* and denotes "a desire" and "the striving for it." Only in the teachings of God can man find his goal and strive for it.

In other words, God sets out His desire for His creation. Only in the study of His instructions and teachings can you learn these desires and strive for them. For instance, Chaim learned that it was God's desire for His creation to live humbly; by studying this instruction, he began to strive for this humility.

That is why the Torah is so important to Jewish life and thought. It is not a set of rules and regulations that will cause God to strike you down with a bolt of lightning if you mess up just one. The law of God is your instruction manual on how to live that teaches you God's desires. Why would you not *chapats* or *delight* in it?

In the LXX, the Greek word used to translate *chapats* is *thelēma.* Like *chapats,* it means *wish, delight,* or *desire* and, most often, *will.* It's mostly used to describe the will of God (see Matthew 6:10; John 6:38; Romans 15:32) and sometimes the will of man (see 1 Corinthians 16:12; 2 Peter 1:21). *Thelēma* refers to what one desires to see brought to fruition; hence, it is not hard to see why sometimes, in antiquity, it meant *determination.* In this sense, Psalm 1:2 and one's "*delight*" in the law of God refers to the individual's wish, will, and determination to carry out the will and desire of the Lord.

Do you know the desire of the Lord for your life? Do you have a determination to strive for it? When Chaim's dad taught him to study God's law, that's all it took for him to know the heart of God and pursue it with his whole heart.

Pray this from your heart:

Make Your desires known to me, oh Lord, that I may strive for them with determination and pursue the will You have for Your creation.

45

A FULL REWARD FOR GENUINE OBEDIENCE

The Lord repay you for what you have done,
*and a **full reward** be given you by the Lord,*
the God of Israel, under whose wings you
have come to take refuge!
—Ruth 2:12

I found nothing but superiorities in myself and this explained my good-will and serenity. When I was concerned with others, it was out of pure condescension, in utter freedom, and all the credit went to me: my self-esteem would go up a degree.
—Albert Camus, *The Fall*

Albert Camus's book, *The Fall*, is a pretty sobering read. It's about a guy named Jean-Baptiste Clamence who talks to you, the reader, about his heyday in Paris, when he was rich, successful, and had, above all things, a good opinion of himself. The story goes downhill quickly from there. He starts to tell you how a number of events in his life signaled to him that he was a duplicitous person. He began to realize that all the good deeds he did served some ulterior motive.

For example, when Clamence helped a blind man across the street, he tipped his hat to the fellow, a gesture the other could not see. Clamence comes to grips with the fact that he did it for the passersby who were watching him help the man. He wanted to impress them with his kindness. Before you know it, you start to feel bad for Clamence. He's tormented by his own double-dealing, and he has no peace. His story may even make the reader feel anxious. There's a lot to take away from the book.

Reading *The Fall* as Christians, we may find ourselves asking why we do what we do. Is there any reward in deeds done out of self-interest or vain ambition? Can doing things with a greasy palm satisfy us with peace?

If we are going to talk about the reasons why we do what we do, it's good to consider the book of Ruth. Ruth is said to have been blessed with a "*full reward*" for her deeds. The Hebrew word *reward* here is *maskoreth* from the root word *sakar,* meaning "wages" or "payment in return for services that are rendered." However, in its Semitic origins, it is used for "a dam causing water to fill a basin." In other words, it has the idea of filling a *void,* an *emptiness,* or a *need*. The word *full* in Hebrew is *shalomah,* the feminine form of the word *shalom,* which is the Hebrew word for *peace*. Thus the blessing Ruth was to receive would fill a void in her life, but that fulfillment would also bring her *shalom* or *peace*. She would not only find a husband to care for her—which was the goal of a woman in that culture—but she would have the added bonus of a husband who would love her and cherish her besides making her life peaceful. Most men in those days did their duty as a husband, but not all did so out of love and a longing to bring happiness and fulfillment to their wives. Ruth's end was peace, which is quite different than the experience of our antihero, Jean-Baptiste Clamence.

In the LXX, the Greek word used to translate *maskoreth* is *misthos*. A very common word in the New Testament, it means "wages," "renumeration," and "an agreed salary." It's what you get for performing a service. Jesus talks about rewards in the Sermon in the Mount:

> *Beware of practicing your righteousness before other people in order to be seen by them, for then you will have no reward from your Father who is in heaven. Thus, when you give to the needy, sound no trumpet before you, as the hypocrites do in the synagogues and in the streets, that they may be praised by others. Truly, I say to you, they have received their reward. But when you give to the needy, do not let your left hand know what your right hand is doing, so that your giving may be in secret. And your Father who sees in secret will reward you.* (Matthew 6:1–4)

If you'll allow us to be anachronistic, the hypocrites Jesus talks about are like Clamence. They are fraudulent. The charity they perform isn't to serve others or even to honor the Lord; rather, they seek to have others honor them. Jesus says those who do this have no true reward. But those who do their good deeds with a pure motive—not to receive a reward in return—will receive a full reward from the Father: their lives will be filled with the peace (*shalom*) of knowing God.

The Jewish Midrash and the Talmud spend a considerable amount of time discussing this issue of rewards filling a void with peace. The sages teach that there is no reward for keeping the law of God. This is something we should just do out of love for Him. Ruth was a Moabite who converted to Judaism. She voluntarily submitted herself to the laws of God. She did not have to do this. She just loved God and wanted to obey His laws. Since she did it for no reward, Boaz blessed her by declaring that God would reward her.

The Midrash sets forth a principle that the most desirable component in doing a virtuous deed is the service of the heart.

In the Talmud, Sanhedrin 106b, we learn that God desires good deeds to flow from the heart out of love, not the expectation of reward. Sure, we know all this, but do we really understand what it means? How often do we try to bribe or manipulate God with good deeds? Maybe we do a favor for someone or put money in the offering plate and think, "Well, now God will mark that up to a good deed when I make my bid for heaven."

But keep in mind, Ruth asked for none of this. She only wanted to take care of her mother-in-law, to do what was right for the two people she loved the most: Naomi and God. God's *sakar/misthos,* reward or payment, was not expected.

When you serve God, are you doing it with your heart in your hand or with a greasy palm?

When Jews speak of obeying the commandments and law of God, they say they are performing a *mitzvah.* This basically means "a good deed." Although the literal meaning for the Hebrew word *mitzvah* is *commandment,* the word really expresses a sense of heartfelt sentiment beyond mere legal duty. Instead, a *mitzvah* is done out of love for God, not out of obligation or an effort to bribe or manipulate God.

Sometimes, Jewish people are accused of not believing in heaven or an afterlife. Chaim can affirm that Jews definitely believe in a heaven, although they have different words for it, such as *garden of Eden, paradise,* or even *the afterlife.* But they do not speak about heaven very much because they want to focus on their mission here on earth. They sort of let heaven take care of itself and focus instead on fulfilling their mission and purpose in life, without the expectation of some reward.

Once you start talking about heaven and trying to get there, you have to consider whether all of your good deeds and good works are being performed just to get you there.

So, here's a question: why do you do what you do? Maybe there's a little Clamence in all of us. Maybe, like the religious hypocrites of Jesus's day, we do what we do to impress not just the public but also ourselves. Sometimes our own supposed acts of charity and humility cause us to think that we are the favored of God and entitled to something good. If that's the case, those double-dealings need to be laid at the cross. They must die. Like Ruth, our obedience must be because it is the right thing to do—period. God will handle the reward. Leave that to Him. Our focus needs to be on what is right for the sake of doing what is right. Full peace accompanies that.

Pray this from your heart:

May my motives be pure, oh Lord. Let no guile or double-dealings be found in my obedience to Your commands.

46

A CONJOINED HEART

Woe to them, for they have fled from Me! Destruction to them, because they have ***transgressed*** *against Me! Though I redeemed them, yet they have spoken lies against Me. They did not cry out to Me with their* ***heart*** *when they* ***wailed*** *upon their beds. They assemble together for grain and new wine, they rebel against Me.*
—Hosea 7:13–14 (NKJV)

Let's say you get one of those letters from the IRS, and you know you're in big trouble. What do you do? Well, you do what any self-respecting, born again, evangelical Christian would do—you pray, and you pray earnestly. "Oh, Lord, I know I don't go to church as much as I should. You know that. And I only pray to You when I am in trouble, and boy, am I in trouble now…" That little prayer is the best illustration we can think of for Hosea 7:14. It is a perfect example of crying unto God, but not with the heart.

The prophet Hosea is prophesying to the Northern Kingdom during the reign of Jeroboam II in the eighth century BC. This is the time just before they were taken into captivity by the Assyrians. In the hopes of appeasing the Assyrians, Jeroboam encouraged the worship of Baal, their god. He also tried to gain a little more security by introducing calf worship with the aim of winning an alliance with Egypt to fight off the Assyrians. But when famine hit the land, guess who the Israelites turned to? The same one you turn to when all your other gods fail you.

This is where Hosea comes in. Hosea married an unfaithful woman named Gomer. He was really in love with her too! When Gomer ran off with other men and became destitute, Hosea would take her back, only to have her run off with another man yet again. This is so like the Northern Kingdom.

This is what is being expressed in Hosea 7:13. God comes to the Northern Kingdom's rescue but they soon transgress against Him. The Hebrew word for *transgress* is *sur,* which in its Semitic root means "to withdraw." How often do humans tend to withdraw from God when problems are no longer looming, when the IRS is paid off or the lump has disappeared? The attitude seems to be, "Okay, God, see You next time I need You."

The key problem in Hosea is not that the people are calling out to God in time of trouble. The verse says they wailed from their bed. To howl or wail to God shows sincerity in your need and focused attention on God. It seems that the worst moments of our struggles come in the middle of the night when we are trying to sleep. Some of the sincerest prayers that we pray are offered when our anxiety wakes us up in a panic at 3 a.m. On many nights, Chaim has tossed, turned, and prayed to the Lord until sunrise. "I'm not going to stay up all night praying unless I am being sincere!" he declares.

But despite the Northern Kingdom's late-night prayers, the Bible says they didn't call upon God with their hearts. This is a bit hard to reconcile. Surely someone sitting up in bed in tears, with their arms raised to heaven while crying out to God, giving Him their full attention, must be crying from their heart!

Nope. According to Hosea 7:14, apparently not.

The word *heart* in Hebrew is *levev.* In its Semitic root, *levev* conveys the idea of cojoining, like two twins who are joined in some physical way together at birth. They could share similar organs, body parts, or even a head.

We often view the heart as the center of our emotions or feelings. And this is true. It's our emotions and feelings, our heart, that joins us to others. It also joins us to God. When we offer our feelings and emotions to God, we become conjoined with Him. Our heart shares His heart, and His heart bonds with ours.

It's possible to pray sincere, panicked prayers without ever offering our hearts to God. This happens when the driving force behind our fright-riddled midnight prayers is a sincere desperation for help…but without any interest in the One we are calling on for help. They are "sincere" prayers in the sense that they contain sincere fear, dread, or sadness. But they are insincere in the sense that they contain no real concern for the Lord.

Welcome to the Northern Kingdom.

In the LXX, we discover that the Hebrew word *levev* is translated as *kardia,* the common Greek word for heart. *Kardia* means "the inner self," "the center," or "interior." This word is used a lot in the New Testament, which has a great deal to say about the inner nature of humans. In the Gospel of Mark, perhaps there is an echo of Hosea 7:14 and the issue God was having with the Northern Kingdom. In this passage, Jesus is quoting Isaiah 29:13:

> *And he said to them, "Well did Isaiah prophesy of you hypocrites, as it is written, 'This people honors me with their lips, but their heart (kardia) is far from me"* (Mark 7:6; see also Matthew 15:7–9)

While this is language from Isaiah, it does go hand in hand with Hosea. It is not too far of a stretch to suggest that maybe Mark's audience would have thought of Hosea and Gomer's situation and the trouble God was having with the Northern Kingdom during that time. Be that as it may, this passage, and Jesus quoting it, indicates just how prevalent it was for God's people to make a sincere case with their lips but never have any real sincere connection or bond with God. They were prayers born from self-interest that their survival instincts led them to pray, without any interest in the Lord that could have enabled them to share God's heart and know Him.

We can reconcile it like this: there are two ways to be sincere—either sincere about what's best for you, or sincere about serving the Lord as He brings about what's best for you. Gomer was interested in herself, not Hosea. The Northern Kingdom was interested in itself, not God. And the religious leaders of Jesus's day were interested in themselves, most certainly not Christ. The funny thing is, they all knew how to move their lips and pray, especially in times of trouble.

The next time your panic wakes you up at 3 a.m. and you are lying there wailing on your bed, think of God. Do you just want a quick fix? Or do you want your heart to bond and connect with God's heart as you seek Him in the trouble?

Pray this from your heart:

I offer You my sincerity, oh Lord. May my heart bond and connect with You as I seek You for those things I need.

47

GROWING IN OUR WALK

*Though I **walk** in the midst of trouble, you preserve my life;*
you stretch out your hand against the wrath of my enemies,
and your right hand delivers me.
—Psalm 138:7

When Chaim was a young boy, his dad was always going for long walks. The family owned a cottage in Northern Michigan, and Chaim's childhood was filled with times of keeping up with his father on trails through the dunes. He still remembers the ache in his legs from trying to last a few miles with his dad, who encouraged him by saying, "Come on, son, toughen up those legs. You can do it." Chaim would always push through. Walking with your father is special when you're a young boy, even if you have to deal with aching muscles.

In Psalm 138, David is talking about walking with the Lord.

Chaim was a little surprised when he read this verse in Hebrew. He fully expected to find the word *halakah* for *walk* but instead he found the word *yalak*. Both words might have similar origins, but they do have different roots. Thus, they can both mean *walk,* but each is a different type of walk. *Halakah* is a righteous walk. Chaim assumed that if he walks a righteous walk in the midst of trouble, God will preserve him.

In other words, you can expect help from God only if you are walking a righteous walk and you suffer for His name's sake.

However, the *yalak* is the Hebrew word used for *child* or *youth*. In its Semitic origins, it has the idea of "giving birth" or "bringing forth." This creates a picture of innocence, of a child who acts foolishly without thinking of the consequences. Then when confronted, he begins to regret his foolishness.

More to the context, however, Chaim found in Jewish teaching that *yalak* is also a child learning to walk—sort of like a young boy learning how to walk beside his dad.

There's a tradition for every milestone that a Jewish child reaches, a tradition meant to teach us about our development and growth in our relationship with God that parallels that of a child growing and maturing.

When it comes time for a Jewish child to learn to walk, it is the father who teaches the child. He stands the child in front of him, moves a few feet away, holds out his arms, and says, "Come to your dad for a hug." The child, so anxious for that hug, forgets he cannot walk. He just follows his natural instincts and moves toward his father.

That's sort of like how it was for Chaim as a young boy. He was so anxious to be next to his dad that he forgot about the pains in his legs. He just kept up with his father so he was walking like him.

It's not too much to imagine that Psalm 138:7 depicts God showing us how we should learn to walk a righteous walk. It comes out of the eager desire to walk the way Jesus did. We are so desirous to be near Him that we instinctively find ourselves living like Him.

When we come to the LXX, we discover that the Hebrew word *yalak* is translated into the Greek word *poreuomai*. There's genuinely nothing peculiar about this word—in fact, quite the opposite. It is so common that it is easily overlooked. It probably would not be included in a Greek word study. What's exciting about a word that means "go," "to travel," or "to make a journey"? It really has no wider use in the New

Testament than that. However, it *becomes* interesting when we being to notice just how many times, out of all its uses, it is used by Jesus. (See Matthew 10:6–7; 11:4; 22:9; 28:19; Mark 16:15; Luke 5:24; 7:8, 22, 50; 8:48; 10:37; 13:32; 17:14, 19; 22:8; John 4:50; 8:11; 20:17…just to name a few.) It is clear that *going* is one of the main themes in the Gospels. It's quite important to Jesus. Whenever He commands someone to *go*, there is going to be a result!

Perhaps the most well-known verse out of the aforementioned is the one in which Jesus commands the woman who was caught in adultery to *go* and sin no more:

> *Jesus stood up and said to her, "Woman, where are they? Has no one condemned you?" She said, "No one, Lord." And Jesus said, "Neither do I condemn you;* ***go****, and from now on sin no more."*
>
> (John 8:10–11)

In another widely known instance, a sinful woman wets Jesus's feet with her tears, wipes them with her hair, and anoints them with precious oil. She is condemned by the Pharisees for it, but Jesus forgives her sins. *"And he said to the woman, 'Your faith has saved you; go in peace'"* (Luke 7:50).

In both of these instances, Jesus is telling these women to walk. Like whom? Like Him. He's saying, "Keep up with Me!" They'd have to learn and they'd have to grow, just like a child whose unsteady steps become sure as time goes by. But the eager desire in both women would cause them to keep up with the Lord, to obey His words, and to live like Him.

Yes, we are called to walk righteously, to be like Christ through our obedience to His words. But let's not ever forget that this begins by being like a child who just wants to walk with his dad.

This eagerness begins in us when the Holy Spirt first convicts us of sin. That conviction puts in us a desire to walk in a different direction, the direction Jesus is going. You'll find that eagerness moving you to follow Jesus all the way till the end of your life. You'll have times when you fall and bang your knee. Maybe you'll even have times when you stop and think about giving up. But because Jesus has called you to walk with Him, He will be faithful to bid you to keep walking. Let a childlike eagerness push you forward to walk righteously with the Lord.

Pray this from your heart:

Lord, I am eager to walk with You, like a child who walks next to his father. May I be righteous in the way I live, keeping Your words through my obedience.

48

OLD, WORN, AND SHATTERED TO BITS

My flesh and my skin hath he made ***old;***
he hath ***broken my bones.***
—Lamentations 3:4 (KJV)

Why not? They are the only ones who can take it.
—C. S. Lewis, when asked why the righteous suffer

Tradition ascribes the book of Lamentations to Jeremiah, who is said to have written this book just as Judah fell to the Babylonians. If you take a trip to Israel, your tour guide may take you to the cave where Jeremiah lived while writing Lamentations. Perhaps it's true. But chapter 3 is more of a personal refection than a lament over Judah. Jeremiah should have been rejoicing over the fact that his prophecies have proven true, but after all, it was his home and homeland that had fallen. There was no joy in this vindication.

One thing we can say for sure is that God could never be sued for false advertising. He clearly points out in His Word that the righteous will suffer, and it is through those fires that they are purified as gold.

A good example of the righteous suffering can be found among the early saints from the fourth century who participated in the Council of Nicaea in AD 325. The council's major accomplishment was confirming the deity of Jesus. The council also established the Nicaean Creed, which is still used as our statement of faith and belief.

The Council of Nicaea was convened by the emperor Constantine, who invited 1,800 bishops throughout Europe to attend. Only 318 showed up. These were not beautifully robed, pompous church officials such as we might envision. Just twelve years prior, Constantine and the emperor Licinius had issued the Edict of Milan, which ended the horrendous persecution of Christians in the Roman Empire. These 318 bishops who attended the Council of Nicaea were survivors of this persecution. Among them, 306 were missing one or more of their physical limbs—arms, hands, legs, or feet—or eyes. All bore physical evidence of the torture they endured for refusing to deny their faith in Jesus Christ. They boldly traveled to Nicaea and confirmed their common belief. The Nicaean Creed declares that Jesus Christ is the Son of God and was born of a virgin, died on the cross for our sins, and rose from the dead. That was the first order of business, and it was established as the foundation of the church. These delegates clung to this belief at great sacrifice and personally witnessed friends and family who died clinging to this belief.

If we cannot endure suffering, then these bishops who attended the First Council of Nicaea had something that we do not have.

Jeremiah states in Lamentations 3:4 that *he* makes my flesh grow old and *he* breaks my bones. *He* is referring to God. The word *old* in Hebrew is the verb *bilah,* which is in the Piel perfect form. It would more appropriately be rendered as "waste away in terror." In the LXX, the Greek verb used to translate *bilah* is *palaioō.* It means "to make old" or "decay through lapse of time." It is used a few times in the New Testament.

In one instance, Jesus warns His disciples against pursuing material things and exhorts them to instead store up treasures in heaven. He says, *"Provide yourselves with moneybags that do not grow old"* (Luke

12:33). These moneybags were little drawstring pouches that were used for carrying money. These moneybags would wear out, and valuables would start dropping out of them. This reminds Chris of an old Bible he had for more than ten years and read every day...until the pages started to fall out. It looked like it had been run over by a truck.

Every so often, the news media will show before and after photos of past presidents of the United States. Most of the presidents display tremendous signs of aging after only a couple years in office. It is a common belief that the stress of the office ages a person. That is *bilah* in a Piel form; it is *palaioō* taking place in a human. Their face and hair are as worn as an old money sack or a vintage Bible. Jeremiah aged like this, before his time, due to the stress he was under in the office of a prophet.

We also learn that God broke his bones, which we believe is a metaphor. The Hebrew word for break is *shavar,* which is in an intensive form, so God did not just *break* Jeremiah's bones but *painfully* broke them into splitters. That'll make your toes ache. This Greek rendering of this word in the LXX is *syntribō.* (Doesn't that just *sound* like a word that hurts?) It means "to smash," "to shatter," "to crush," "to annihilate," and "to grind down." In antiquity, the word was used to describe breaking the bones and smashing the skulls of animals. In the New Testament, it is used to describe something being obliterated by force, such as the alabaster flask containing ointment that a woman *"broke"* (*syntribō*) to pour over Jesus's head. (See Mark 14:3.) The flask was shattered and broke to bits.

Now we have a picture of Jeremiah's suffering: worn by age, shattered into tiny little pieces.

Did God inflict a painful breaking of Jeremiah's bones? Did He painfully break the bones of the 318 delegates to the Council of Nicaea? In a sense, yes. By choosing to believe and love God, these men suffered great affliction. Had they not chosen God, they could have enjoyed a peaceful life. But they chose obedience instead.

Elizabeth Clephane wrote a poem entitled "Beneath the Cross of Jesus" that could have been dedicated to Jeremiah, the 318 members of the Council of Nicaea, and millions of other Christians. We pray that we too can claim these words as well:

I take, O cross, thy shadow
For my abiding place:
I ask no other sunshine than
The sunshine of his face;
Content to let the world go by,
To know no gain nor loss;
My sinful self my only shame,
My glory all the cross.

As our culture becomes more and more hostile toward God, we will find that obeying God will become less and less convenient and comfortable. There might be a time, sooner rather than later, when it will cause our skin to be made old and our bones to be broken. Will we be like Jeremiah and the bishops at the council of Nicaea? Time will tell…

Pray this from your heart:

I desire to obey You, oh Lord, even if my bones are shattered and I'm ground to nothing. Give me the grace to suffer for Your name.

49

IS IT VAIN TO SERVE THE LORD?

Your words have been ***stout*** *against me, saith the* Lord.
Yet ye say, What have we spoken so much against thee?
Ye have said, It is vain to serve God: and what ***profit*** *is it that we have kept his ordinance, and that we have walked mournfully before the* Lord *of hosts?*
—Malachi 3:13–14 (KJV)

A few old cartoons depict cowhands and wagoners dangling carrots attached to sticks in front of their horses. The horse never gets to eat the carrot. It's just a cruel trick to keep the animal moving forward.

This gives us an illustration of what is going on in Malachi 3:13–14.

The Lord said, *"Your words have been* ***stout*** *against me."* The Hebrew word for *stout* is *chazak,* which comes from a Semitic root meaning "to be stubborn." This means you resist any help or any attempt to change your course of action. In the LXX, the Greek word for *chazak* is *baryon,* which means "to burden," "to weigh down," or "oppress by weight." The root of the word is *baros,* which means "a burden." Paul uses it when he tells the Galatian church, *"Bear one another's burdens"* (Galatians 6:2). The burden literally means a heavy stone one is required to carry a long way. Figuratively, it meant a person's trials. If one were to speak burdensome words, these words would be heavy, having the ability to weigh one down. They are stubborn, oppressive words. We get the picture of a complainer, firm in their whining protest. Ever meet someone like that?

Chaim recalls going on a hike with his family. One of his cousins got so tired of getting dragged through the woods that they started to complain and whine until they finally snapped and refused to move another inch until everyone promised to head back home. Their stubborn protest made a nice day heavy and miserable for the whole family.

When you are on a stubborn protest, no amount of reasoning will alter your direction.

Malachi records that the people of God, in their stubbornness, deny complaining to the Lord. "What have we spoken against You?" they asked. These are words from the heart. In this context, these words would be very meaningful and powerful. They wanted to know, "What have we said that is heavy and a complaint?"

But God calls them out on their heart. They believe *"it is vain to serve God."* They don't believe that there is profit in keeping His ordinances. And they've said this to the Lord. Why is this such a horrible thing to say to God? Because their attitude is, if we do not get what we want, then it's not worth serving the Lord.

This can be the trap of Western Christianity. It's the idea that as long as we pay our tithe and put money into the offering, we are going to have a really happy, financially blessed life.

Yet how do we account for the bankruptcy court being filled with Christians who have paid their 10 percent plus in tithes faithfully? Western Christianity is littered with the dry, sunbaked bones of Christians who have faithfully served God and kept His commandments and yet ended up turning against God because they were not adequately blessed or paid for all their efforts.

This is "serving God" with sense of entitlement. They ask, "How has keeping His ordinance profited us?"

The Hebrew word for *profit* is *batsar,* which means "to plunder" or "to gain at the expense of another."

If you, as a righteous person, bid for a job against an unrighteous person, wouldn't you expect to get the job because you are righteous? And if you don't get the job and the other person gets it through dishonesty, would you throw up your hands and say, "So what did all this honesty get me anyway?" Basically, in Malachi 3:14, the people are saying that those who keep the laws of God should profit over those who don't.

In LXX, the Greek word used to translate *batsar* is *pleiōn,* meaning *numerous* and *large*. It is part of a word family that describes being *full*. But there are words in this family that have a negative sense and mean *greediness*. (See 1 Thessalonians 2:5; 2 Peter 2:3; 2:14.)

The tone in Malachi 3:14 suggests that the people feel entitled for keeping God's ordinances. They greedily expect a blessing from God for doing what they were supposed to be doing in the first place.

If we have this attitude while giving, how is giving to the house of God any different than investing in the stock market with the expectation that we will be paid a dividend every quarter?

It is obvious what the prophet is saying here: It's a great sin to serve God and keep His commandments in order to get richly paid or blessed for doing so. But there is something more to it than that. If we believe such a thing about God, we are accusing God of deception. We are suggesting that God is like the wagon driver dangling a carrot in front of the horse to get it to move with no intention of letting the horse have the carrot. We are saying God is dangling all these promises of riches and blessings to get us to obey Him and live a good life, but He never intends to make good on these promises. This is why it is so horrible to ask, "Is it vain to serve God? What profit is there in keeping His laws?"

There was a story recently about a twenty-nine-year-old woman who married an eighty-five-year-old man worth a billion dollars. Of course, his money had nothing to do with it. What we are really saying if we have the attitude found in Malachi 3:14 is, "God, I will love You so long as You pay me, but if the paychecks ever stop coming in, then I will just find myself another god who knows how to take care of me."

Can we honestly say, "God, if You go broke tomorrow, and You are no longer the great Provider," we, like Job, would still trust Him? (See Job 13:15.) Some of us may have to face that test just to be sure of why we love Him.

There is a scene in *Fiddler on the Roof*[5] where Tevye is reflecting on the marriage of his daughter Tzeitel to Motel and sighs, "They're as poor as squirrels in winter. But, they're so happy, they don't know how miserable they are." If we are truly the loving bride of Christ, then God does not need to dangle a carrot in front of us to get us moving; we do so simply because we love Him in sickness and health, for better or for worse, though richer or poorer. And if He chooses to allow sickness, poverty, and the worst to come into our lives, we will still be so happy, we won't know just how miserable we are because we are content in His grace.

Pray this from your heart:

I obey You for obedience's sake, oh Lord. I humbly accept Your blessings and grace as a gift, not something I am entitled to. My heart belongs to You in spite of what I get or what I lose.

5. *Fiddler on the Roof,* directed by Norman Jewison (1971; United Artists).

50

GOD ALLURES US

*Therefore, behold, I will **allure** her, and bring her into the wilderness, and speak tenderly to her.*
—Hosea 2:14

As a child, Chaim was terrified that he wasn't saved. He would constantly pray the sinner's prayer and hope he said the words right. He would try with all his might to repent, but still never feel that assurance that everyone talked about. If he came home from school and no one was home, he would quickly turn on the radio to listen to the local Christian radio station, and if they were still broadcasting, he knew that the rapture had not occurred and he was not left behind.

One day, Chaim read a book in which someone expressed the same concern. She said she would pray constantly to be saved and try with all her might to repent, but never *felt* saved. The author said something he will never forget: "God wants you a million times more than you want Him."

Ever since that day, Chaim has searched the Scriptures for confirmation of that statement—and almost every day, he has found that confirmation. God does indeed want us a million times more than we want Him. Probably even more.

This brings us to Hosea 2:14. In this passage, the Hebrew word for *allure* is *pathah*. It means "to open" and "to loosen." It is also a word used by warriors who draw their swords. In ancient times, when two armies confronted each other, they would wait for someone to make the first move, to draw the sword.

Even today, when a world crisis occurs, the United States will send in its powerful naval and military aircraft to flex its muscle, so to speak. But they will not fire one shot unless the other side does. The hope is that the other side will be so intimidated, they will back down. This is what is behind the word *pathah*. In ancient times, as the two armies faced each other in the wilderness or battlefield, each side was waiting for the other to draw their swords or *pathah*. They would insult each other, insult their nation, insult their king or their gods, tell them their mothers wear combat boots, or yell similar taunts. Then suddenly, someone would shout, "What did you say about my momma?" And he would draw his sword and the fight would be on.

However, in the context of Hosea 2:14, *pathah* is trying to draw another person into an encounter or loving relationship. It is not exchanging insults to get a response, but rather words of love and longing, seeking an embrace and an exchange of love.

In the LXX, the Greek word used to translate *pathah* is *planaō*. It means "to lead astray," "to deceive," and even "to seduce." It is used in Revelation 2:20 to describe Jezebel who *seduced* (*planaō*) the servants of God in Thyatira to practice sexual immorality and participate in idolatry. The idea this word holds here is seduction and enticement and, perhaps a less pejoratively, *wooing*, which is how this word is being used in Hosea.

The picture in Hosea 2:14 is God taking His people out to the wilderness and speaking words of love to them. The words *"speak tenderly"* refers to Him speaking His heart. He is not doing this out of a self-absorbed egotism. Rather, He speaks His heart out of His commitment to them.

It reminds Chris of the time his friend taught him how to write a love letter. Chris was a college freshman in Minneapolis, Minnesota. The girl of his dreams lived back home in Michigan. And this was in early 2003, before Facebook or Instagram or text messaging was even a thing! Chris missed this girl. He would look out the window at the Minneapolis skyline, see the snow falling on the IDS Center and steam rising from sewers, and think that somewhere beyond this metropolis was the girl who held his heart. His buddy said, "Why don't you write her a letter and put your heart into written words?" So Chris sat down at his desk, under fluorescent lights, sort of the way he would if he were writing a theology paper. His buddy read the letter and threw it in the trash.

"Man, you know what your problem is?" Chris's friend asked. "You aren't wooing her in this. You are talking like a scholar." He turned on a warm, retro lamp, turned off the fluorescent lights, and had Chris sit on the couch. Then he gave Chris a leather journal and handed him a cup of tea. "Now, chill, brother," the friend said. Then he put on some alluring music. And guess what? The lined journal started seeping up the oozing *allure* dribbling out of Chris's pen. He was trying to draw the girl into a loving relationship by speaking words of love to her heart from his heart. And these words communicated his care and desire for commitment. This is *pathah/planaō*.

And believe it or not, as sappy as it sounds, this is what's going on in Hosea 2:14.

Today, we do well to remember the love, care, and commitment that God has for His people. This is especially true when our own hearts seem to be far from the Lord, like in times when we have become too busy to pay any attention to God, or in those times when we have made some pretty boneheaded mistakes. God is merciful. He will always offer grace before judgment. He's kinder than we probably even realize, and He allures us to repentance by the conviction of the Holy Spirit. It is our proper response to receive this allurement, to be enticed by it, and to offer our commitment back to Him.

Pray this from your heart:

I offer my commitment to You, oh Lord, as a response to Your allurement. Your love and commitment to me are great, and I respond with my vow to be faithful to You.

FINAL WORD

Our hope is that these fifty studies have drawn you closer to the heart of God. We pray they enable you to live faithfully to Christ through obedience to His Word.

Moreover, it would be no small thing if these studies have produced in you a desire to explore Scripture through the biblical languages. The Bible is an entire world. The ancient languages in which it was written help you notice things in that world you might've otherwise missed. Certainly, our English translations are good. But the original languages can draw you closer to the text. If you find that desire growing in your heart, we encourage you to pursue it. Somewhere along the line, that desire sprung up in both of our hearts. And we're sure glad that we honored it. You'll be glad too.

The ultimate end of a Bible study is to know God and produce fruit unto Him. Whether you study the Scriptures in English or the original language, we leave you by praying for you as Paul prayed for the Colossians:

> *Asking that you may be filled with the knowledge of his will in all spiritual wisdom and understanding, so as to walk in a manner worthy of the Lord, fully pleasing to him: bearing fruit in every good*

work and increasing in the knowledge of God; being strengthened with all power, according to his glorious might, for all endurance and patience with joy. (Colossians 1:9–11)

ABOUT THE AUTHORS

Chaim Bentorah teaches biblical Hebrew, Aramaic, and Greek to lay teachers and pastors in the metro Chicago area through Chaim Bentorah Ministries. He also speaks to church and parachurch groups about the nature and means of studying the Old Testament in the original Hebrew. His books combine a devotional emphasis with scriptural studies into the deeper meanings of Hebrew words.

Chaim and his study partner, Laura Bertone, write daily word studies on their blog at www.chaimbentorah.com. They are also the copastors of a cyber Messianic church through their subscription All Access online at HebrewWordStudy.com, on which they conduct twelve-week classes in basic Hebrew, a weekly Monday evening Bible translation class, and a Sabbath Torah study on Saturday mornings that follows the Parshah (Weekly Torah Portion).

Chaim has a bachelor of arts degree in Jewish Studies from Moody Bible Institute, a master's degree in Old Testament and Hebrew from Denver Seminary, and a PhD in Biblical Archaeology. All of his Hebrew professors in college and graduate school were involved in the translation of the New International Version of the Bible. In their classes, he learned of the inner workings involved in the translation process. In graduate school, he and another student studied advanced Hebrew under Dr. Earl S. Kalland, who was on the executive committee for the translation work of the New International Version. It was this committee that made the final decisions on the particular renderings used in the original NIV translation.

Having done his undergraduate work in Jewish Studies, Chaim was interested in the role of Jewish literature in biblical translation. Professor Kalland encouraged him to seek out an orthodox rabbi and discuss the translation process from a Jewish perspective. From this experience, he discovered many things about the Hebrew language that he had not learned in his years of Hebrew studies in a Christian environment. Later, from his contact with Jewish rabbis and his studies in the Talmud, the Mishnah, and other works of Jewish literature, as well as his studies in the Semitic languages, Chaim began doing Hebrew word studies as devotionals and sending them out by e-mail to former students whom he had taught in his thirteen years as an instructor in Hebrew and Old Testament at World Harvest Bible College, as well as those he taught through Chaim Bentorah Ministries.

In addition to several self-published books, Chaim is the author of *Hebrew Word Study: Revealing the Heart of God; Hebrew Word Study: Exploring the Mind of God;* and *Journey into Silence: Transformation Through Contemplation, Wonder, and Worship.*

Chris Palmer is the dean of TheosU and Theos Seminary, a Greek scholar, and a professor of theology. He edited and co-authored *Theos Starter Pack: Toward a Recovery of Essential Christianity*. He also authored *Winks from Scripture: Understanding God's Subtle Work Among Us*; *Greek Word Study: 90 Ancient Words That Unlock Scripture*; *Letters from Jesus: Studies from the Seven Churches of Revelation*; and *Strange Scriptures: Deciphering 52 Weird, Bizarre, and Curious Verses from the New Testament*.

Chris is currently working on his PhD at the University of Wales, Bangor (UK).

Chris has travelled to more than forty nations and has helped many congregations grow, flourish, and expand. His desire for missions is to train and educate pastors, encourage congregations, support the vision of the local church, and show the love of God to the culture. He has worked successfully with both traditional churches and the underground, persecuted church.

You may find Chris online at www.chrispalmer.me.